Praise for Overcoming Generational Curses

"This book is a collection of stories of tragedy that should have never happened. It reveals many unspeakable acts that affect all of us as a society. The stories show how much society turns a blind eye and a deaf ear to child abuse. Orgeron shows with great skill the devastating effects of child abuse. As is often the case, her abuse was ignored. I am glad she told her story, shared what she has learned through her pain, and used it to encourage others."
—Sandra Krug, CRNA, ARNP, RRT, Legal Nurse Consultant, Certified Mental Health First Aid Instructor, Certified Professional Christian Life Coach, Certified DISC Profile Analyst (CDPA)

***

"In her latest book *Overcoming Generational Curses,* author Pamela Orgeron does a fabulous job addressing the long overdue issues of "destructive family secrets," which affect more people than we could ever imagine. The author shares the searing pain of growing up keeping family secrets day after day and how the consequences of carrying those secrets set her up for dysfunction in her personal life. After many years of prayer, faith, and research, she developed a step-by-step plan to overcome the pain that had changed her life. Her trust in her Savior Jesus Christ is obvious as she uses Scripture to back up every step in this journey. She reflects a love for God and a love for people in every chapter of this must-read, life-changing book."
—Barbara Ward, CONNECT Group (Sunday school) Teacher, First Baptist Church, Hendersonville, TN

Additional Praise

"As I read this book, I found myself saying; 'That was really helpful', and 'I wish someone I know could read this'. Another obvious realization was how this book can help those among us who are hurting or stuck in personal growth because of generational curses or addiction. I also found it confirming and reinforcing many of the values and experiences in my journey. This is life-changing information to the many challenges to living now."
—Eugene (Gene) H. Benedict, M.A., LPC-S, San Antonio, Texas

***

"*Overcoming Generational Curses* came as a ray of hope in the dark subject of child abuse. It reveals how often child abuse is denied and the victim is blamed instead; increasing the victim's pain. It reveals the generational curses that began the problem and leads us forward to overcoming by allowing God to move us. This is a great book for victims, survivors, and those of us who want to help the victim realize that they can overcome generational sin."
—Sandra K. Henry (Thompson), Retired English Teacher, Fairview High School, Ashland, KY

***

"Such a beautiful testimony written by Pam Orgeron! She's so transparent and vulnerable throughout these pages. It's almost like you're sitting with her at a coffee shop, listening intently as she captivates your attention with her words of wisdom. Such a wonderful author; her writing style is unique as she shares her life on these pages."
—Rebecca Devernoe, BCMHC, BCPC, South Florida Bible College Enrollment Advisor, Deerfield Beach, FL

OVERCOMING GENERATIONAL CURSES: Finding Freedom in Truth, A 3-Step Process

OTHER BOOKS BY PAMELA K. ORGERON:

The ABC's of Life for Children and Adults: Short Stories, Essays, and Poems Promoting Christian Concepts (Xulon Press, 2003)

The New ABC's of Life for Children and Adults: Short Stories, Essays, and Poems Promoting Christian Concepts (ABC's Ministries, 2016)

We Survived Sexual Abuse! You Can Too! Personal Stories of Sexual Abuse Survivors with Information about Sexual Abuse Prevention, Effects, and Recovery (ABC's Ministries, 2016)

Food as an Idol: Finding Freedom from Disordered Eating (ABC's Ministries, 2017)

A Legacy to Remember: "Recollections of a Common Man" (ABC's Ministries, 2018)

Food as an Idol: The Types, Causes, Consequences, Conquering, and Prevention of Disordered Eating (ABC's Ministries, 2019)

Why Didn't They Hear Us? The Causes, Consequences, and Solutions to Children Feeling Unheard (Author Academy Elite, 2020)

***

OVERCOMING GENERATIONAL CURSES: Finding "Freedom in Truth", A 3-Step Process

Written by:
Pamela K. Orgeron, M.A., Ed.S.
BCCC, ACLC, BCMMHC, Speaker, Author

ABC's Ministries
Nashville, TN

Overcoming Generational Curses: Finding "Freedom in Truth", a 3-Step Process. Copyright © 2024 by Pamela K. Orgeron. All rights reserved.

Library of Congress Control Number: Pending
ISBN PB 978-1-7342245-0-4; HB 978-1-7342245-1-1; E-book 978-1-7342245-2-8

Printed in the United States of America

No part of this publication may be reproduced or transmitted in any form or by any means without written permission of the author or publisher.

Unless otherwise indicated, Bible quotations are taken from New King James Version. Copyright © 1982 by Thomas Nelson, Inc.

"…For I, the Lord your God, *am* a jealous God, visiting the iniquity of the fathers upon the children to the third and fourth *generations* of those who hate Me, ¹⁰ but showing mercy to thousands, to those who love Me and keep My commandments." (Deuteronomy 5:9-10, NKJV).

Dedication

This book is dedicated to all my cousins and other extended family members who no doubt have their own scars resulting from the sins of our forefathers. To each one I say, I love you. My prayer is that each one of you will choose to break through any denial in your life and choose to take the road to recovery. May God's will be done in each of your lives.

TABLE OF CONTENTS

Preface	xv
Acknowledgments	xvii
Introduction	xix

Step One:
Breaking Through Denial and Revealing the Truth

1. Generational Curse Versus The Blessing	3
2. False Beliefs of Dysfunctional Families	9
3. It only happens in the movies! Wrong!	15
4. Digging Out the Dirt "Family Secrets"	20
5. Reasons Perpetrators are Protected	25
6. Are Victims to be Blamed?	30
7. Hanging on to Denial? Let it Go!	35

Step Two:
Healing the Consequences of Generational Curses

8. Protective Factors for Victims of Trauma	43
9. Nehemiah . . . A Biblical Basis for Recovery	48
10. Overcoming Through Therapy, Coaching, and Support Groups	53
11. Education…a Door to Recovery	57
12. Healing through Prayer	62

13. Healing through Scripture	68
14. Healing through Writing and Other Creative Arts	78
15. Forgiveness, Grieving the Losses, and Reparenting through Positive Self-Talk	82

**Step Three:
Moving Forward and Allowing God to Use You**

16. Remember Relapse Happens	89
17. Stay Focused	94
18. Be Aware of Your Weaknesses	100
19. Utilize and Focus on Your Strengths	105
20. Be an Advocate for Others	111
21. Above All, Sow in the Spirit, NOT the Flesh	116
22. Final Reflections: "Good Triumphs Evil"	123
Recommended Resources	125
About the Author	131

Preface

With over 3 years of not writing any books, why does the author pick up the pen now? First and foremost, the Lord has placed it on her heart to write *Overcoming Generational Curses: Finding "Freedom in Truth". A 3-Step Process*: This book will help those persons who are suffering the consequences of generational curses. Secondly, the Lord has revealed to the author that the time has come to reveal her identity as the author of the book entitled *Freedom in Truth: My Story of Deliverance and Restoration from Past Abuse and Scandal* (Inspiring Voices, 2019) written under a pseudonym.

Orgeron's writing *Freedom in Truth* was to enable the principles expressed in 2 Corinthians 1:3-4 to be lived out in her life. If her sharing her story will spare other victims of similar incidents from further victimization by families trying to hide similar tragedies, more concerned about reputations than the feelings and needs of victims involved, then her mission has been accomplished. By revealing her identity as the author of *Freedom in Truth*, her purpose is not to hurt her extended relatives or those in the community where she grew up. Orgeron's purpose is to motivate and encourage others to examine their lives to understand the consequences in their lives that resulted from the sins of their forefathers. She encourages other victims to repent of the misdeeds of those before them and to offer forgiveness in their hearts towards the offenders. She can honestly say she has no feelings of anger or bitterness about what happened. God had His purposes for allowing what happened to her and to others in her family and community just as when He allowed Joseph to be sold into slavery (Genesis 37:12-36).

Pamela K. Orgeron

Acknowledgments

First, I want to thank my husband for the love, understanding, and support he has given me since we met. I can't thank him enough for sticking with me through thick and thin during the years we've been married.

Secondly, I want to thank those family members from both sides of my family who have helped, and continue to help and encourage me over the years. Many of those whom are deceased at this time still leave an impact on me through their death. I often find myself asking what my father, his mother, or someone else would do in a particular situation or decision I have to make. When that happens, typically, the Holy Spirit in His still small voice will give me the answer.

Additionally, I also could not have survived without encouragement from my teachers throughout my academic history. A couple of those teachers are current friends whom I respect greatly and whose advice I value highly.

Furthermore, I cannot fail to mention all my former and current pastors and church friends, whom I have been blessed to know through the years. Many of these brothers and sisters in Christ are closer to me than my own biological family of origin.

Lastly, I can't thank my Father in Heaven enough for how He has guided and protected me over my lifetime, as I realize the outcome could have been a lot worse without His presence. He has brought an insecure small town girl to become a confident woman who dedicates the rest of her life for the up building of His kingdom. Thank you, Lord! Without You, I can do nothing. (John 15:5)

***

Introduction

Every family has skeletons in their closets, those "family secrets" no one is supposed to talk about to protect a family name, reputation, or whatever. The author's family is no different. However, any therapist will tell you such secrets, and denying the truth are not healthy.

"The truth is that whatever one seeks to hide and cover up will eventually work its way up to the light and become known — even if it is murders or other crimes..."[1] Furthermore, as Galatians 6:7-8 indicates individuals will reap the consequences of whether they sow in the flesh or in the Spirit.

The Holy Bible offers Scriptural support that "family secrets" always get uncovered, one way or another. These Scripture passages and other favorite passages have given the author peace and/or have inspired her through recovery to seek the truth. They continue to do so as she writes this book that shares ugly skeletons in many closets. These passages include:

"[2] For there is nothing covered that will not be revealed, nor hidden that will not be known. [3] Therefore whatever you have spoken in the dark will be heard in the light, and what you have spoken in the ear in inner rooms will be proclaimed on the housetops" (Luke 12:2-3, NKJV).

"And you shall know the truth, and the truth shall make you free" (John 8:32, NKJV).

"[10] When my father and my mother forsake me, Then the LORD will take care of me. [11] Teach me Your way, O LORD, And lead me in a smooth path, because of my enemies" (Psalm 27:10-11, NKJV).

> *"And we know that all things work together for good to those who love God, to those who are the called according to His purpose" (Romans 8:28, NKJV).*
>
> *"³ Blessed be the God and Father of our Lord Jesus Christ, the Father of mercies and God of all comfort, ⁴ who comforts us in all our tribulation, that we may be able to comfort those who are in any [a]trouble, with the comfort with which we ourselves are comforted by God" (2 Corinthians 1:3-4, NKJV),*

Skeletons in Pam's past include rape, incest, physical abuse, murder, scandal, and other forms of abuse, No doubt the abuse and dysfunction that she has been exposed to over her life goes back a number of generations. (Exodus 34:7; Numbers 14:18; Deuteronomy 5:9; Exodus 20:5) Over time most of the memories dealing with the traumatic experiences of the author's childhood slipped into oblivion, or so people thought. What happened was never discussed openly. Neither did she receive treatment as a child to work through the issues that should have been addressed at that time. When Pam recognized the dysfunctional patterns in her family decades ago, she made up her mind then that by the grace of God and with His help the dysfunction stops with her.

In addition to abuse and trauma in her early childhood, Pam also has experienced a lot of losses over her entire lifetime that impacted her significantly, including deaths, a broken marriage, miscarriage, etc. However, she has had a number of protective factors that no doubt buffered the worst case scenarios resulting from those times of stress and uncertainty.

Overcoming Generational Curses: Finding "Freedom in Truth". A 3-Step Process: is divided into three sections. Articles in the first section deal with the first step of any recovery process. It's entitled "Step One: Breaking through Denial and Revealing the Truth". Articles in part two deal with how individuals can heal from the negative consequences of past sins, whether from one's own past or from the sins of our forefathers and is entitled "Step Two: Healing the Consequences of Generational Curses". In the last section, "Step Three: Moving Forward and Allowing God to Use You", the author shares information about dealing with relapse and offers suggestions about how to move forward from recovery to experience a joy-filled life led by the Holy Spirit.

The author chose to write *Overcoming Generational Curses* in third person to enable herself to remain more objective in her writing. She refers to herself as Pam in the book when sharing stories of herself as a child and during the time before she legally changed her last name from her maiden name of Owens to her married name Orgeron.

Orgeron desires that every person who reads *Overcoming Generational Curses* will find the hope, courage, and the will to dig out the skeletons in the closets of their family and their own closet to break free from the bondage and chains in their lives. It is only by doing this that one can find true freedom and deliverance through Christ. Though Pam's journey to find freedom and healing in discovering the truth was not easy and was with a lot of obstacles along the way, she has no regrets in looking back.

Pamela K. Orgeron
January 4, 2024

Notes

[1] Crudup, Ronnie. "What's done in darkness will come to light." *Clarion Ledger.* June 12, 2015. ¶ 6. Retrieved January 18, 2024 from https://www.clarionledger.com/story/life/faith/2015/06/12/done-darkness-will-come-light/71148142/

Step One: Breaking Through Denial and Revealing the Truth

Breaking Chains to Move Forward

CHAPTER 1

Generational Curse versus the Blessing

Honestly Pam had never heard of parents blessing children until she was a young adult. Looking back, there were those in her childhood who gave her a blessing; although, she didn't know what it was at the time. Unfortunately, many of these blessings were neutralized by curses that she received from the early childhood abuse and trauma that she experienced. Thanks are to God, she has overcome those curses. She gives God all the glory for breaking those curses.

> *In the Bible, blessing refers to flourishing and the multiplication of life. But it doesn't always look like these things, and for many of us, life often looks and feels like the opposite.*
>
> *We look around us and find a broken world filled with suffering, corruption, poverty, and war. We experience chronic illness, family dissension, and addiction. Our minds and bodies endure abuse.*
>
> *For many of us, it feels more real to say life is about suffering than life is about blessing. And perhaps there's a feeling within all of us that something has happened. Something has gone wrong. This is not the way it should be.*

Pamela K. Orgeron, M.A., Ed.S., BCCC, ACLC, BCMMHC

> *The Bible has a name for this kind of dysfunction—the curse.*
> *In the Bible, the curse is when God hands people over to the consequences of seizing blessing on their own terms. It is a curse because, instead of abundance and life, we end up with scarcity, isolation, and death,* [1]

Based on the above citation and other research in general, Orgeron considers a generational curse and a blessing to be on opposite ends of a continuum, opposites in nature. Can generational curses be broken? Here are what writers at Focus on the Family report:

> *Set theology aside for a moment. Common sense tells us that behavior and attitude problems tend to run in families. Just like physical characteristics of height, weight, hair color, and complexion.*
> *In the same way, certain types of sin can pass from generation to generation. This is particularly true of addictive behaviors such as alcoholism. Similarly, physical and sexual abuse might become ingrained in the psychological legacy of certain families.*
> *However, none of this should be viewed in terms of an irreversible "curse." Spiritual deliverance is available to everyone who sincerely calls upon the name of the Lord (Romans 10:13). And there are many sources of professional assistance for those who need practical help — pastors, therapists, counselors, and doctors.* [2]

Without mentioning specific names, Orgeron discusses the generational curses that she is aware of within her family. One of the first generational curses that she thinks of as being in her family is alcoholism. On one side of the family, she was told that her great great grandmother was a full blooded Indian. Research indicates that there is a genetic predisposition for alcoholism within families of the Indian race. As soon as they were old enough to drink alcohol, many of the males in the family picked up the bottle, with a few actually ending up alcoholics.

God only knows when and where the child sexual abuse first originated. When Pam asked her mother about her grandfather's childhood, her mother replied, "We don't know. When we asked him about his childhood, he wouldn't talk about it." Since her grandfather was reported to have said to her grandmother, his wife that he saw nothing wrong with abusing children sexually, Pam suspects his behavior was learned as a child, probably a victim of child sexual abuse himself. As one of Pam's therapists said to her, "People tend to parent in the way that they were parented unless they recognize the dysfunction and make a conscience decision to change."

Disordered eating also was a big generational curse in Pam's family of origin. It was more common in the females of the family. Many of the women in the family were yo-yo dieters, including her mother and her. She was even diagnosed with an eating disorder when she was in her 20s but has repented and since overcame that prior dysfunction in her past.

Contrast blessing with generational curse. What are the components of a blessing?

Throughout Scripture, the blessing always included five key elements:

1. *Meaningful and Appropriate Touch*
2. *A Spoken Message*
3. *Attaching High Value*
4. *Picturing a Special Future*
5. *An Active Commitment*

Pamela K. Orgeron, M.A., Ed.S., BCCC, ACLC, BCMMHC

Each of the elements serves a specific purpose for both the one giving and the one receiving the blessing. [3]

Without any reservations, Orgeron believes the individual who offered her the greatest blessing in life was her paternal grandmother. Her grandmother's love displayed all five key elements of the blessing. How so?

Unlike Pam's immediate family that was not the affectionate type, her paternal grandmother displayed appropriate hugging and tender touches to let her granddaughter know that she was loved by her. That love also reflected through their conversation regularly. She recalls three particular statements that her grandmother said on more than one occasion.

> **"People tend to parent in the way that they were parented unless they recognize the dysfunction and make a conscience decision to change."—Kathy Sherrod, Psychologist**

Orgeron remembers frequently spending the night with her grandmother as a young child. Lying across her grandmother's bed, she remembers telling her grandmother how her mother would beat and verbally abuse her whenever another adult was not around. Her grandmother replied, "Well, you work hard in school and do well. When you grow up, you can leave all the abuse and never have to come back, if you don't want to."

She remembers as a young child replying to her grandmother, "I'd come back to see you."

Additionally, her grandmother also would say, "You're the daughter that I could never have myself." What a loving statement for the grandmother to have said!

The third statement occurred when they would be talking about what Pam might want to do as an adult. Her grandmother said, "You can do anything you want to do as long as you are willing to work for it and it's within God's will." Wow! What a wonderful grandmother-granddaughter bond! What a legacy to leave with a child!

Though Pam's father failed to stand up against his wife for physically and emotionally abusing the children, he too blessed his daughter as a child and even later as an adult. Without his having suggested the "homework first" policy and his encouraging her to do well academically, she would not be where she is today professionally. She remembers her father giving out her spelling words to her in elementary school and how proud he was of her for going to her school's regional spelling bee as the winner of her sixth grade class. In her earlier elementary years, she remembers receiving a dollar for every "A" that she brought home on her report card. After Pam became an adult, her father blessed her by helping her purchase her first car, by paying her college tuition when she was ready to drop out of undergraduate school because of financial reasons with less than a year left to graduate. Later after moving away from home, Orgeron cannot remember the number of times her father would go behind her mother's back to send her extra money. What a legacy he left!!!

Despite her mother's mental illness, in hindsight, Orgeron remembers two specific times when she felt blessed by her mother. The first time was when she was in grade school and her mother told her, "I had it hard growing up. My mother was sick in bed a lot, and with me being one of the oldest left at home, I had to do most of the housecleaning and taking care of the younger children. I didn't like it, and never wanted you to have to go through that. That's why I don't give you chores to do so you can focus on your schoolwork." Though her mother said that, a part of Pam never believed her mother's words because they contradicted how her mother criticized her for not doing things exactly as she wanted them done when she did try to help, Her mother was obsessive compulsive when it came to keeping the house clean. Furthermore, she told her daughter at other times that it was easier for her to go ahead and do something herself rather than to try to teach her daughter. Obviously, Pam received a lot of mixed and contradictory messages from her mother as a child. She attributes that to her mother's mental illness.

The one "incomplete" blessing as an adult that Orgeron will not forget happened during the last year of her mother's life when Orgeron had gone back to Kentucky to spend time with her mother over Mother's Day and her mother's birthday that year. While she was visiting her mother at the nursing home, she tried to get her mother to talk about what happened when the murder she witnessed occurred. At least, her mother acknowledged that it did happen and said, "I'm sorry you were hurt." Although, when pressed further to give details, her mother said, "I don't want to talk about it."

In closing this chapter, Orgeron hopes that by her being transparent in sharing her story, parents, grandparents, and other caretakers of children today will be proactive in offering children a blessing rather than a curse. She would say to them, "Just do it!"

***

Notes

[1] Drimalla and BibleProject Team, What Does the Bible Say About Blessing and Curse? Exploring the Theme of Blessing and Curse in Scripture, ¶s 3-7, https://bibleproject.com/articles/how-does-the-bible-explain-suffering/.

[2] Focus on the Family, Understanding the "Generational Curse" of Exodus 34:7, But what about addiction and abuse? Section, https://www.focusonthefamily.com/family-qa/understanding-the-generational-curse-of-exodus-347/.

[3] Trent, The Blessing: How to Bless Your Child, Key Elements of The Blessing section, https://www.focusonthefamily.com/parenting/how-to-bless-your-child/

CHAPTER 2

False Beliefs of Dysfunctional Families

Author's Note: This article is an updated and edited version of a blog written by the author. The blog was written October 26, 2019 entitled "'Don't Talk': 'Don't Trust'; 'Don't Feel': False Beliefs I Overcame".

Introduction

In any unhealthy, dysfunctional family three unwritten rules exist: Don't talk. Don't trust. Don't feel. Orgeron's family of origin was no different in teaching these unhealthy practices.

Don't Talk

"What happens in this family, stays in this family," Orgeron recalls her father saying once. She doesn't recall all the details of what happened when her father said that. What she does recall is being in trouble for telling an "outsider" something "bad" that had happened in their family. Apparently, the outsider confronted her father about what she had shared with him or her.

Don't Trust

Trusting anyone, even God has been a struggle for Pam in her past. She learned at an early age that some people are not trustworthy, which she projected to everyone, even God as she got older. Growing up with a mentally-ill mother who often contradicted her words and actions, the nature of her illness, Pam found trusting others difficult. Because love and trust go hand in hand, she also found accepting love from others difficult.

When people would talk about how God loves everyone just like our earthly parents, she struggled with this concept, as she felt unloved and unacceptable in her mother's eyes. Nothing seemed to ever be good enough for her mother. Pam unconsciously transferred her feelings and attitudes about her mother to God.

Don't Feel

"Don't cry. You'll upset your mother. "; "Don't cry. It gets on your mother's nerves."; "Don't be mad. You shouldn't be mad." Commonly hearing such phrases at an early age, Pam came to believe generalizing that having any type of feelings was inappropriate. Thus, she learned to stuff and denied her emotions, especially the negative ones, at an early age.

Recovery from False Beliefs

In the spring of 1989 following the aftermath of having fallen down a flight of stairs and crushing her left ankle the previous year, Pam was first diagnosed with clinical depression, anxiety disorder, and codependency. This is when her "official" (with professional help) recovery began. She finds it hard to believe it's been about 35 years now.

PTSD, and later Complex PTSD, was later added to Pam's diagnosis.

Talk Therapy

As a part of treatment for depression, anxiety, and codependency shortly after her initial diagnosis, Pam entered psychotherapy, "talk therapy". This was the beginning of her learning to recognize and unlearn the dysfunctional family dynamic rule, "Don't talk". Initially, she also was encouraged to find a therapy group to join. *No way*, was her thought about joining any recovery group back then.

Over the years Pam has learned to see value in support groups and learned that the process is biblical. Consider the following verses:

> *"Confess [your] faults one to another, and pray one for another, that ye may be healed. The effectual fervent prayer of a righteous man availeth much"*
> *(James 5:16, KJV).*

> *"If we confess our sins, he is faithful and just to forgive us [our] sins, and to cleanse us from all unrighteousness"*
> *(1 John 1:9, KJV).*

> *"Bear ye one another's burdens, and so fulfil the law of Christ" (Galatians 6:2, KJV).*

Pam used to be very uncomfortable sharing her weaknesses with others until she became aware of the above verses and of the dysfunctional beliefs she had been taught as a child. Now she has no reservations sharing her testimony, her story of recovery as a part of her ministry. The above verses, along with 2 Corinthians 1:3-4, give Oregon the freedom to share her story of having been abused, her unhealthy, sinful reactions to the abuse (e.g.: overeating), and her journey of recovery.

Learning Trust is a Must

While on one hand as a child Pam learned to mistrust others, on the other hand, she recalls her paternal grandmother always telling her, "Honesty is always the best policy. Always tell the truth no matter what." Mama's words enabled her to trust her. She was the one person whom Pam trusted as a child without reservation.

Over the years Pam learned to trust others with a lot of difficulties. She projected the dishonest practices of her mentally ill mother onto others. At times she even had trouble projecting the unhealthy attitudes and behaviors of her earthly parents on God, her Heavenly Father. What she has come to know and understand is that the love of God and the love of one's earthly parents and anyone else on earth are different. Thus, she never compares God's love to the love of a parent whenever she witnesses. Like herself, not everyone has healthy, loving parents to be able to grasp that analogy which in some cases may be applicable.

"[5] *Trust in the* Lord *with all thine heart; and lean not unto thine own understanding.* [6] *In all thy ways acknowledge him, and he shall direct thy paths.* [7] *Be not wise in thine own eyes: fear the* Lord, *and depart from evil.* [8] *It shall be health to thy navel, and marrow to thy bones"*
(Proverbs 3:5-8, KJV).

Feelings Matter

The Scriptures are full of verses that report individuals having feelings of all types. Having feelings is a natural part of being human. Although, feelings are a part of human nature, one should not live his or her life based on feelings or emotions. Feelings can be fleeting, coming and going, and can be misleading at times.

> *"He that trusteth in his own heart is a fool: but whoso walketh wisely, he shall be delivered" (Proverbs 28:26, KJV).*

> *"¹² There is a way which seemeth right unto a man, but the end thereof are the ways of death. ¹³ Even in laughter the heart is sorrowful; and the end of that mirth is heaviness" (Proverbs 14:12-13, KJV).*

Personally, the emotion of anger was what Pam feared most as she grew up and what she denied feeling most in her early adulthood years. Told as a young toddler not to be mad or angry, she had assumed that anger was wrong, a sin. That was a misconception on her part. Even the Scriptures tell us to be angry but do not sin (Ephesians 4:26). Christ Himself became angry with the moneychangers and overturned their tables (John 2:13-16).

> **"Although, feelings are a part of human nature, one should not live his or her life based on feelings or emotions."**

Conclusion/Challenge

Talking/sharing about any past abuse, sins, etc. in one's life; learning to trust God and others; and, learning to recognize and address one's feelings appropriately are keys to a successful recovery from any past "hurt, habit, or hang up", if the author may borrow the phrase from Celebrate Recovery, a Christian 12-step group that she has found most helpful in the later years of her recovery journey.

Pamela K. Orgeron, M.A., Ed.S., BCCC, ACLC, BCMMHC

For persons stuck in the false beliefs of "'Don't Talk': 'Don't Trust'; and 'Don't Feel' Orgeron encourages these individuals to let go of these old dysfunctional attitudes, beliefs, and behaviors that hold them back in moving forward with their healing. Only then can anyone find the ultimate healing and peace through Christ Jesus, the Lord and Savior.

***

CHAPTER 3

It Only Happens in the Movies! Wrong!

Author's Note: A large portion of this article has been extracted, updated, and edited from a blog written by the author. The blog was written January 15, 2018 entitled "'Sexual Abuse & Witnessing a Murder . . . It only happens in the movies. Wrong! It happened to me".

> *"If people only knew the damage they did whenever they molest someone, especially a child, they'd never do it. They'd never do it!" Elaine Baker, PhD, who was my professor of Human Sexuality at Marshall University, Huntington, WV, said (1984).*
>
> *Little did I realize the significance of Dr. Baker's statement to my life until years later whenever I realized I had been a victim of early childhood sexual abuse. Maintaining healthy relationships had always been difficult for me. I could not understand why until I broke through denial and chose to take the long road to recovery.* [1]

When Pam first heard Dr. Baker's statement and description of the symptoms of a person who has experienced past sexual abuse, she thought, *she's talking about me.* At that point Pam contemplated deeply to understand why she exhibited symptoms of sexual abuse. The only memory she could recall at that time was of a co-worker at McDonald's, her first job, trying to rape her. Thankfully, he was unsuccessful due to another employee showing up at the scene. She assumed that was the source of her symptoms and continued to work towards completing her undergraduate work.

Fast Forward About Four Years

Sunday, June 26, 1988… by that time Pam had completed her undergraduate work, lived in Nashville, Tennessee and was a member at Two Rivers Baptist Church. Life was good. However, Pam learned that day how quickly circumstances can change. On her way to church that evening she fainted and fell down a flight of stairs crushing her left ankle. Ten days later July 6 doctors performed surgery that included a bone graft from her hip and the insertion of 2 metal plates and 16 screws to rebuild her ankle. Doctors told her that she would probably never walk again. They said if she did, she would have to use a cane. As is evidenced now by her being able to walk without a cane and even run at times, she knows The Great Physician can heal when modern medicine fails. Throughout her recovery after the accident, she struggled with depression but didn't seek help at that point. Then November 12 of the same year her paternal grandmother passed away. Her death hit Pam hard as she was still in a cast and unable to return to Kentucky for her grandmother's funeral.

Less than 6 months after her grandmother's death, May 9, 1989, her cousin the late American country music entertainer Keith Whitley died. At the time of Keith's death, Pam was feeling exceptionally low, even to the point of contemplating suicide.

"If you have a problem…It doesn't have to be alcohol and drugs . . . any problem, whether it's alcohol, drugs, psychological, or emotional, get help," said Ricky Skaggs, country music artist during Keith's funeral. "Don't let this happen to you. I know this is what Keith would want me to say."

The words spoken by Ricky penetrated deep into Pam's soul. Shortly after Keith's funeral, she sought professional help. Doctors diagnosed her with Major Depressive Disorder, Anxiety Disorder, Codependency, and PTSD from the fall down the stairs. However over time after much prayer and psychotherapy Pam realized that there was more behind the development of PTSD than the accident falling down the stairs: the young man at McDonald's was not her first perpetrator. For example, there was a neighborhood boy who raped her at the tender age of three years of age. There were others too.

Making Sense of Her Life Struggles

"What you are talking about, what you are describing is Complex PTSD. Have you read the book *Complex PTSD* written by Pete Walker?" The late H. Norman Wright, M.A., D.Min. said to Orgeron Friday evening, Sept. 29 at the Grief, Crisis & Disaster Networking Mixer at the American Association of Christian Counselors 2017 Break Every Chain Conference. The author had just given the late Dr. Wright a brief account of a new realization of another trauma in her childhood and its after effects.

Flashback to Saturday, August 19 about six weeks earlier: Sitting at her computer catching up on email and the latest news about her friends at Facebook, Orgeron read that a first cousin had died not long ago. *Oh, no, why didn't someone let me know?* she thought to herself. Sadly, she whispered to herself, "Paul is gone. Paul's gone." This statement to her triggered the new memory of her witnessing a murder as a very young child about 3.5 to 4 years of age. The murder victim shared the same first name with her cousin. With that was the beginning of what psychologists call an emotional flooding experience. She began sobbing uncontrollably as she flashbacked to various memories indicating that she witnessed the beating of a childhood friend, a 16 year old boy, who was coming to the defense of his younger sister whom the perpetrator was trying to rape.

Orgeron remembered as a young child she even tried to save the boy's life before the perpetrator grabbed her and threatened to kill her if she told anyone what happened. She remembered running off in shock and unable to talk for several days. The perpetrator left the boy in the field to die. Others tried to cover up what happened. Not her. She wanted to testify. She was told she was too young. The perpetrator got off on a mentally incompetent defense. The doctor said he had hardening of the arteries and wasn't responsible for his actions. Pam knew that wasn't the case. She saw what happened. She witnessed how angry he was at being caught trying to molest the girl. He had every intention of killing the boy: and, Pam honestly, believes he would have killed her had she not ran when she did.

How does a child so young recover from such trauma? Pam's father did his best to try to give her closure after the final hearing regarding Paul's murder. Her father died February 17, 2016. Before closing this chapter Orgeron shares an excerpt from a therapeutic letter she wrote to her father August 28, 2017:

> *Seeing what happened and experiencing what I experienced hurt me and stole my childhood. I know you thought you were giving me closure when you took me to the scene of the crime to tell me I could not testify and to forget what happened. Closure for me would have been allowing me to testify and grieve Paul's death. I know the last thing*

you asked me at the end of our talk was, "Are you mad at me?" I said, "No". We both collapsed into each other's arms crying. After that I was always "Daddy's girl".

So, one can easily see from Pam's past experiences that tragedy does not only happen in the movies, but they happen in real life. For those persons reading this book who remember experiencing such tragedies but have never received treatment, Orgeron recommends these individuals seek out help to recover. To parents who have a child tell them of such atrocities, please believe the child. Don't try to hide the truth. Get the child professional help as soon as possible. That's the right thing to do.

"...'Let the little children come to Me, and do not forbid them; for of such is the kingdom of God" (Mark 10:14).

***

Notes

[1] Orgeron, P. K. (2016). *The New ABC's of Life for Children and Adults: Short Stories, Essays, and Poems Promoting Christian Concepts.* Nashville, TN: ABC's Ministries, p, 160.

Pamela K. Orgeron, M.A., Ed.S., BCCC, ACLC, BCMMHC

CHAPTER 4

Digging Out the Dirt "Family Secrets"

If one comes from a family where everyone is committed to shoving "family secrets" under the rug, how can one learn the truth? As the old saying goes, "Where there's a will, there's a way."

The first thing Pam did was to pray and ask God to reveal the truth to her about why she felt so different and outcast from others around her. Here are some of the tools God used and continues to use in revealing the truth to her:

- **Personal backflashes.** Warning: If an individual reading this book is experiencing backflashes without being in the care of a professional psychiatrist or psychologist, Orgeron recommends this person get treatment as soon as possible.
- **Historical research through libraries and calling official legal authorities.** Pam called the police from her hometown where she grew up to request records about when she was raped. The officer on the phone told her that because both the victim and perpetrator were juveniles, those records were sealed. She didn't like the officer's answer; although, his answer confirmed that the rape had actually occurred and was not her imagination. Furthermore, to confirm the rape memories, one of Pam's former therapists told her that she was 3

years old when it happened. Apparently, after she had signed a release for her father to be able to talk to her therapist, Pam's father told the therapist about what happened to her as a child.
- **Questioning other older family members privately in subtle ways.** On one occasion when Pam was visiting back in Kentucky and she was at an aunt's house without her mother, she seized the opportunity to ask a lot of questions of two aunts and three older cousins about her mother's relationship growing up with her grandfather. All the answers given pointed to the only thing Pam could conclude: her grandfather sexually abused her mother too.
- **Reports of incidents regarding other family members.** After Pam remembered her grandfather attempting to molest her, a relative told her that one of her older cousins had admitted to having been sexually abused by someone when she was very young. However, the cousin would never name her abuser to the relative but the cousin's brother confirmed suspicions that it was their grandfather. Both of these cousins are now deceased so Orgeron has no problem sharing this information.
- **Questioning older close friends or co-workers of family members.** Just last year Orgeron was communicating with an old family friend who worked with her father. The man revealed to her that her father had confided in him about her grandfather's abusing her and all. The old family friend spoke of how hurt Pam's parents were by what happened. She assumes since her father passed years ago, the old family friend felt telling her the truth was appropriate.

Just recently a friend of Orgeron's shared about a "family secret" in her family. She also gave Orgeron her permission to share the story in this book. The friend told

Orgeron that her great-grandfather had been killed by another man who also got off because of his having a friend in law enforcement. Out of curiosity, Orgeron's friend asked her mother to write a letter and write down everything she knew about what happened. Through the letter Orgeron's friend learned that her great-grandfather's murder was never reported and that his brains (He was shot in the head.) and what was left of him were buried in the back yard. Suspicions were that the murder was over a woman. However, since the victim was married, what happened to the man was never discussed in the family. Orgeron's friend's mother told her daughter, "We don't talk about that."

Years ago Orgeron remembers one woman telling her how one of her great uncles (her grandfather's brother) molested her as a small child. When she told her adopted mother, really her biological grandmother, about what was happening, she was told, "Oh, you can't tell anyone. Keep it a secret. It would hurt your dad too much if he knew what his brother was doing to you." Such stories where no thought was ever given to the child's feelings or well-being should infuriate anyone.

Orgeron does offer a few words of caution to those persons digging into their family's past history because of a family member, even one's self, having indicators of past early childhood abuse. She recalls a number of reactions that different family members displayed. These reactions include denial, anger, resistance, and rejection. Remember multiple reasons for denial exist. One is that the person may actually know the truth about what happened but might lie to protect the family name or reputation. Others deny the truth because they really don't remember what happened or were not told what happened when it happened.

A number of Pam's relatives remained angry with her for years. A couple of them made threats of beating her up if they ever saw her again.

Resistance might surface if the relative being questioned or confronted is too close to what happened. Perhaps that relative was a co-conspirator or accomplice after the fact to what happened and finds facing his or her own guilt difficult. Fear of knowing the truth might also result in resistance.

Some resist answering questions and discourage a person looking back out of pure motives. For example, when Pam first went into therapy her father almost begged her not to look back. Why? He knew the truth and how much it would hurt her. He didn't want to see her in that much pain. Orgeron believes it was out of ignorance that her father did not understand that only through looking back and learning the truth could she find true peace and contentment to move forward.

Orgeron has read about and heard a number of stories where family members rejected the "whistleblowers" in a family. Some victims have been completely disowned by their families for exposing "family secrets" long buried.

Despite all the risks of negative fallout in families, Orgeron still encourages victims to look back and discover what has been eating at them inside. Why? Mental illness is progressive. If a person does not look back to deal with whatever happened, that person runs the risk of developing far worse symptoms that could result in far worse problems. For instance, Pam's mother refused to go to therapy to face her past. She lived a miserable life and made the lives of those around her miserable. Orgeron remembers coming home from school finding her mother sitting on the front porch crying for no reason. Her mother really had few close friends, at least, not that visited their home regularly. Sure, there were all those people she went to church with but like Pam's mom, many of them had their own skeletons in their own closets. That was the culture of the small town Pam grew up in: People did whatever they had to do to protect a family or church's name and reputation. The author will delve deeper into those issues in the next chapter regarding perpetrators.

To conclude this chapter, Orgeron shares a key Scripture verse that encouraged her to look back and dig out what was eating at her deep inside. She hopes the verse encourages others contemplating doing the same. Here's that verse:

> **"If a person does not look back to deal with whatever happened, that person runs the risk of developing far worse symptoms that could result in far worse problems."**

"And you shall know the truth, and the truth shall make you free" (John 8:32).

***

CHAPTER 5

Reasons Perpetrators are Protected

Orgeron believes that those who fail to report perpetrators should be made just as accountable for covering up any generational sin as the perpetrators themselves. Her beliefs are based on the many stories she has heard of where church members have reported to their church that a church member was molesting children. What these church members reported is that the suspected perpetrator was merely excommunicated from the church with no report filed to the appropriate authorities leaving the person free to molest other children outside the church. Other times churches may just sweep the abuse allegations under the rug to not lose financial contributions made to the church by the perpetrator.

Within a family, Orgeron knows from personal experience how perpetrators will be protected. In "Chapter 4: Child Victims Silenced by 'The System'" of her last book entitled *Why Didn't They Hear Us? The Causes, Consequences, and Solutions to Children Feeling Unheard* (Author Academy Elite, 2020) she shared her story:

> *To protect the innocent, I won't be going into detail sharing specific information about other victims involved, etc. What I will share about is how my voice was silenced and some unfair principles I*

have had to accept and face in my recovery from what happened.

To summarize what happened, at the age of about 4 years old I was a key witness who wanted to testify to a horrendous crime that was covered up by relatives, crooked lawyers, and others who were bought off to silence my voice and the voices of other children who witnessed the crime and who also wanted to testify. How did this happen?

"You're too young." Taught by my paternal grandmother that honesty is always the best policy, I wanted and was determined to testify and tell the truth. However, I wasn't permitted to because people said, "She's too young. She doesn't know what she is talking about."

About the other children and me who witnessed the crime, other people said, "They're so young. They'll forget about what happened. It would be their word against his word. Who would believe the children?" Thus, the voices of the children involved were silenced for decades until as an adult I recalled the memories and was able to share the truth, which set me free from years of anxiety, PTSD, and other emotional and psychological wounds that resulted from all the pent-up pain and anger from what happened.

Money talks. Unfortunately, the young ages of the other children involved and myself were not the only factors that contributed to us children's voices being shut down. The perpetrator had contacts with wealthy individuals who paid off the local judge "to make the case go away".

Though what happened was repressed and even forgotten by some over time, I believe God always gets the last word. In Scripture we are told

"²For there is nothing covered that will not be revealed, nor hidden that will not be known.³ Therefore whatever you have spoken in the dark will be heard in the light, and what you have spoken in the ear in inner rooms will be proclaimed on the housetops" (Luke 12:2-3, NKJV).

Yes, my voice was silenced for decades but eventually the truth comes out. (pp. 18-19)

Another writer, speaker, and survivor Miranda Pacchiana, MSW wrote on article entitled "Reasons family members side with sexual abusers" as a part of the Stop Abuse Campaign. She proposed four reasons why others may protect perpetrators

- Denial
- Abuse in Their Own Past
- Fear or Awe of the Abuser
- They Are Perpetrators. [1]

In hopes of helping others struggling with the "why" questions, Orgeron shares a few of the "why" questions that she has struggled with on her journey of recovery. She will discuss possible answers, which she believes were revealed to her by the Holy Spirit.

Why did her grandmother stay with and protect her husband who was abusing her children all those years? One possible logical reason is based on the time period that they lived. Her maternal grandparents lived in a time period where there were no women's shelters or social services organizations that could have helped her. Her grandmother had no safe place to go to take her children.

A second possible reason for Pam's grandmother protecting her husband may be attributed to the phenomenon known as Stockholm syndrome, or "trauma bond". What is Stockholm syndrome?

"... (I)t describes a deep bond which forms between a victim and their abuser.

Victims of abuse often develop a strong sense of loyalty towards their abuser, despite the fact that the bond is damaging to them." [2]

Orgeron attributes Stockholm syndrome as a root cause of her grandmother's protecting her husband based on her grandparents' story, which Orgeron remembers hearing straight from her grandmother when she was a young teenager. Here is what her grandmother told her: Her grandmother was 14 years old and her grandfather was about 26 years old when they married. Her grandmother first told Pam of how she and her grandfather first became friends. Then he wanted to have sexual relations with her. She was taught that premarital sex was wrong so she refused his advances. When she refused, he said, "Let's get married then".

Her grandmother's parents did not approve of the relationship because of the age difference and told them that it would never last. She was determined to prove them wrong. When they would not sign for her to get married, she said that she ran off and swore out a lie that she was 16 years old. "Our marriage wasn't legal from the beginning," her grandmother said, "but became what's known as a common law marriage after so many years." It is not difficult to see how Orgeron would surmise that the grandmother too was a victim of her husband, a child molester; thus, attributing Stockholm syndrome as a reason behind her allegiance to him.

Why did Pam's father not protect the children more by forcing his wife to get professional help? The counselor in Orgeron attributes two main reasons to her father's not standing up to his wife: his having low self-esteem and the counsel of his mother. Her father's low self-esteem she attributes to the fact that her father was an adopted child having been given away by his biological mother.

What was the counsel of Pam's paternal grandmother that she remembers overhearing? As a young child Pam remembers accompanying her father to her grandmother's house for a visit. While there, the two adults were discussing all the problems in the family. Her father told his mother that he and his wife were talking about divorce. "Now, Marvin, you know our family doesn't believe in divorce. You made your bed. Now you have to lie in it," she replied.

Why did Pam's mother not support her in telling the truth about the evil she had witnessed? For one of the very same reasons that she attributes to the maternal grandmother protecting the perpetrator, Stockholm syndrome! In addition, Pam's mother was always concerned about putting on appearances and not ruining the family's reputation or name.

To conclude this chapter, Orgeron writes to those reading this book that are protecting perpetrators, especially at the expense of hurting others, please tell the truth. That is the right thing to do.

***

Notes

[1] Pacchiana, Reasons family members side with sexual abusers. Retrieved January 10, 2024 from https://stopabusecampaign.org/2019/03/23/reasons-family-members-side-with-sexual-abusers/

[2] Ivison Trust, What is trauma bonding? ¶s 1-2, Retrieved January 11, 2024 from https://ivisontrust.org.uk/child-sexual-exploitation/what-is-trauma-bonding/

Pamela K. Orgeron, M.A., Ed.S., BCCC, ACLC, BCMMHC

CHAPTER 6

Are Victims to be Blamed?

Blaming survivors may result from a worldview that attempts to reckon with and rationalize unjustifiable situations. The contradiction between what one wants to be accurate and what is true can make some people feel defensive. Defensiveness and disbelief might lead to accusations, doubt, and placing responsibility on someone who has experienced trauma.

Empathy and connection are effective tools against these tendencies. A mental health professional can also support those being unfairly blamed or wanting to change their mindset about abuse. [1]

Orgeron understands how others can be falsely blamed for something as the victim. She remembers how her mother blamed her for being raped at the tender age of three years old. In a conversation she remembers overhearing her mother have with a couple of aunts about the rape, she recalls her mother saying to her aunts, "I blame her. She brought it on herself. She's too sweet to the boys." How wrong her mother was to put that blame on a child so young!

Why do people like to blame victims? In an article she wrote for *Psychology Today*, Juliana Breines, Ph.D., a social and health psychologist, suggests "5 Reasons Why People Blame Victims" [2] These reasons follow: The first reason proposed is to minimize one's own vulnerability in thinking what ever happened could happen to them. These victim-blamers say the victim did something wrong to bring on the offense and that by not doing whatever the victim did, they will be safe.

The second reason is that observers might physically distance themselves from victims due to social stigmas or strong religious convictions. For example, a person placing a high emphasis on purity might see a rape victim as "damaged goods"; thus, avoiding any social contact with the person.

Breines also proposed that a person's empathizing with or having a closer connection to the perpetrator might prompt one to minimize blaming the person really at fault, the perpetrator. Orgeron thinks this reason would be another reason to apply to her grandmother who stood up for her husband over her granddaughter's desire to tell the truth.

Fourthly, observers objectify the victim. In such cases, they say the victim's dress or other appearance justified an attack.

Lastly, Breines shared that some individuals may just enjoy victim-blaming. They might have a sadistic nature.

Orgeron knows many of the perpetrators in her life story were victims themselves. If children grow up in an incestuous environment where sexual relations between an adult and child was the "norm" and the children were never taught that sex outside of marriage between a man and his wife was wrong, can those children really be blamed for continuing those behavior patterns into their adulthood? Pam has wrestled with that question. In general, she would say the individual situation of the adult victim perpetuating the abuse would determine whether he or she was to blame. In her grandfather's case, assuming he grew up being sexually abused as a child, Orgeron firmly believes he is to blame. He failed to take responsibility for his actions and stop the pattern when confronted by both his wife and leaders in the church. He had been told and knew better. Yes, she believes he was to blame!

Besides other persons blaming a victim, sometimes a victim will blame him or herself for what happened, resulting in a lot of shame and/or false guilt.

> *...The root causes of the false guilt felt by those abused are deeply rooted in our brains.*
>
> *Even though abuse is never a survivor's fault or within their control to stop it, trauma-related guilt often stems from a feeling that a survivor could have done more to prevent what happened to them, stopped it, or fought back.* [3]

Orgeron has experienced a lot of false guilt in her life since remembering the murder she witnessed as a young child. On her road to healing and recovery she has asked questions such as, was there anything more that she could have done to have saved the boy her grandfather had beaten up and left to die. Logically, in her mind, she knows that as a 4-year-old child back then, the situation was out of her control. She could have done nothing more than what she did to try to save the teenage boy's life. By the time she could talk to tell anyone what really happened, a number of days had passed. It was too late to save the boy. However, knowing that does not keep her from doubting her actions back then and asking the "what if" questions.

Who was to blame for the teenager's death? Orgeron believes that not only does blame fall on her grandfather who committed the murder; but, blame also goes back to the church elders who failed to report the "accusations" against her grandfather years before. Had the church leaders reported the "accusations" and her grandfather been in jail where he belonged, that teenage boy who died might still be alive today. Additionally, a lot of other children might have been spared a lot of trauma from abuse from the grandfather.

Orgeron also experiences a lot of what is known as "survivor's guilt", in regards to two of her older female cousins who have passed on. One of those cousins admitted having been sexually abused by an older person. Unfortunately, due to the poor choices she made and not having God in her heart growing up, she fell into promiscuity, alcohol and drugs, and even spent time in a women's prison. No doubt, she died an early death due to the generational curse on her life.

In hindsight looking back, Orgeron firmly believes that the second female cousin who died an early death also became a victim to her grandfather's grasp, as she too displayed many indicators of someone sexually abused in early childhood.

> *"Even though abuse is never a survivor's fault or within their control to stop it, trauma-related guilt often stems from a feeling that a survivor could have done more to prevent what happened to them, stopped it, or fought back."* — The National Foundation to End Child Abuse and Neglect

Why did Pam not end up like her two cousins who died early deaths? What made the difference? Orgeron believes the biggest difference lies in the fact that she recalls inviting God into her heart at a young age. With the Holy Spirit in her heart, the choices she made were more conducive to her overcoming the abuse and trauma in her past to live the full productive life that she lives now.

***

Notes

[1] BetterHelp Editorial Team, Why do people blame survivors of abuse and trauma? Takeaway written at end of article, Retrieved January 11, 2024 from https://www.betterhelp.com/advice/abuse/why-do-people-participate-in-victim-blaming/

[2] Breines, 5 Reasons Why People Blame Victims, Retrieved January 11, 2024 from https://www.psychologytoday.com/us/blog/in-love-and-war/202309/5-reasons-people-blame-victims

[3] The National Foundation to End Child Abuse and Neglect (EndCAN), Banishing Guilt and Shame from Childhood Abuse, Why Abused Children Can Feel Shame and Guilt section, ¶s 1-2, Retrieved January 11, 2024 from https://endcan.org/2021/10/04/banishing-guilt-and-shame-from-childhood-abuse/

CHAPTER 7

Hanging on to Denial? Let it go!

Though she knows some will disagree with her, Orgeron believes that there is no good reason for anyone to stay stuck in denial about an offense or trauma that has occurred. What is denial? Kendra Cherry, MSEd, a psychosocial rehabilitation specialist, psychology educator, and author, defines denial in the following way:

> *Denial is a type of defense mechanism that involves ignoring the reality of a situation to avoid anxiety. Defense mechanisms are strategies that people use to cope with distressing feelings. In the case of denial, it can involve not acknowledging reality or denying the consequences of that reality.* [1]

How does one recognize denial in one's self or others? Heidi Godman, Executive Editor, *Harvard Health Letter* reported:

> *People in denial often exhibit certain behaviors. For example, they might*
>
> • *minimize or justify problems, issues, or unhealthy behaviors*
>
> • *avoid thinking about problems*

- *avoid taking responsibility for unhealthy behaviors, or blame them on someone else*

- *refuse to talk about certain issues, and get defensive when the subjects are brought up.* [2]

Orgeron remembers her struggles with denial when she first began having backflashes to past sexual abuse. She did not want to face what happened. Why? She had always considered herself a virgin and her sexual purity was important to her. She had always intended to save herself for the man she hoped to someday marry. *If the memories that surfaced were true, that means I'm not a virgin,* she thought sadly.

How did Pam come to break through her denial to face reality? She remembered something her mother had said to her in grade school when she shared with her mother how neighborhood boys had molested her. After the incident where the neighborhood boys molested her, Pam could not shake the guilt she was feeling and expressed this to her mother.

"Just remember, in God's eyes, you are still a virgin because it wasn't something that you wanted or brought on yourself," her mother told her. Hearing that statement gave Pam as a child peace about what happened. Remembering that statement as an adult helped her break through the resistance she felt about moving forward in her early days of recovery.

Initially Pam stayed silent about what she remembered in her past because of embarrassment and fear of what others might say. Additionally, her therapist at the time suggested that she only talk about what happened in "safe environments" without her family around, especially until she was further along in her healing process and was strong enough to accept any rejection that might follow by her disclosing the truth.

Are there other reasons survivors choose to remain silent about abuse? Brittany VanDerBill in an article at *PsychCentral* reported:

> *Survivors of abuse may not tell anyone about the abuse for a variety of reasons, including:*
>
> • **Judgment.** *Sometimes, a survivor may be afraid that other people are going to negatively judge them.*
>
> • ***"No one will believe me."*** *They might think nobody would believe them if they did tell someone that they were abused.*
>
> • **Safety.** *A survivor may be very afraid of their abuser and may fear for their safety if they open up about their experiences. It can be common for abusers to threaten their victims to keep them silent.*
>
> • **Fear of punishment.** *A survivor may be afraid to say anything due to potential punishment, such as if someone is abused by a supervisor at work, a parent or caregiver, or someone in a place of authority.*
>
> • **Shame.** *Shame can play a significant role in keeping survivors silent. Survivors may believe that the abuse was somehow their fault or that they caused it. They might also feel embarrassed or ashamed that they didn't or couldn't defend themselves.* [3]

Regardless of what dark skeletons people find in their forefathers' closets or in their personal closet, breaking through denial to accept what happened and taking responsibility for their recovery process is crucial to living a healthy productive life.

> "'Just remember, in God's eyes, you are still a virgin because it wasn't something that you wanted or brought on yourself,' her mother told her."

Breaking through denial is not always easy, and sometimes life will seem to get worse through the initial stages of recovery. However, life does get better over time and is worth any distress of working through the truth of what happened. Again, Orgeron reminds victims what God's Word teaches:

> [31] *"Then Jesus said to those Jews who believed Him, 'If you abide in My word, you are My disciples indeed.* [32] *And you shall know the truth, and the truth shall make you free'"* (John 8:31-32).

Orgeron wants victims to know that God loves them and can heal damage from any trauma. Not only does God want to heal victims, but He can redeem the damage done from abuse when denial is broken through. If you doubt her words, consider the following Scripture:

> [25] *"So I will restore to you the years that the*
> *swarming locust has eaten,*
> *The crawling locust,*
> *The consuming locust,*
> *And the chewing locust,*
> *My great army which I sent among you.*
> [26] *You shall eat in plenty and be satisfied,*
> *And praise the name of the* LORD *your God,*
> *Who has dealt wondrously with you;*
> *And My people shall never be put to shame* (Joel 2:25-26).

Since breaking through her denial and choosing to move forward to find peace in the truth, Orgeron praises God for how He has blessed her, restoring the years that the locust had eaten. She believes God will do the same for anyone coming to Him in repentance seeking the truth. To those persons reading this book in denial, she encourages them to just let "it" go.

***

Notes

[1] Cherry, Denial as a Defense Mechanism, ¶1, Retrieved January 12, 2024 from https://www.verywellmind.com/denial-as-a-defense-mechanism-5114461#:

[2] Godman, Denial: How it hurts, how it helps, and how to cope, Spotting behavior patterns that suggest denial section, Retrieved January 12, 2024 from https://www.health.harvard.edu/blog/denial-how-it-hurts-how-it-helps-and-how-to-cope-202307262958

[3] VanDerBill, Why Abuse Survivors Stay Silent, Reasons abuse survivors might stay silent heading, Retrieved January 12, 2024 from https://psychcentral.com/health/silent-about-abuse

Step Two: Healing the Consequences of Generational Curses

With learning…
the Sky ⇧ is the Limit!

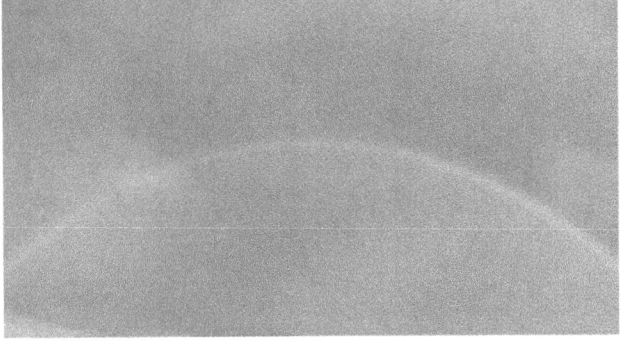

CHAPTER 8

Protective Factors for Victims of Trauma

Orgeron first used the term "protective factors" in the book *Freedom in Truth*. Protective factors would be those factors that keep a person from ending up with the worst case scenario in terms of consequences following a trauma or sinful action. In *Freedom in Truth* she identified her paternal grandmother's presence, the presence of God, scriptural encouragement, prayer, and a love of learning as protective factors in her life growing up. To those protective factors, in this book she adds two more things to the list. The first item is the support of honest, caring individuals and groups of individuals. The second factor Orgeron adds that can help neutralize damage from generational curses is for an individual to possess resilience.

> "Protective factors would be those factors that keep a person from ending up with the worst case scenario in terms of consequences following a trauma or sinful action."

Who were the individuals in Pam's childhood who served as protective factors helping to buffer the damage from the generational curses in her life? First, there were other relatives on both sides of Pam's family besides her paternal grandmother who protected, encouraged, or at least tried to help her in some form or fashion. She remembers, for example, when she was in early grade school and her mother was in the psychiatric hospital having shock treatments, two of her aunts, her mother's sisters, stepped up to help look out for Pam. Both aunts have passed but Orgeron will never forget the kindness they showed to her at that point in time. Additionally, one of those aunts had a daughter about 6 years older than Pam. Orgeron refers to her as the big sister whom she never had. This cousin was an excellent role model for Pam doing well academically and who also genuinely cared for the younger cousin. The two cousins stayed close until Pam moved to Nashville. Shortly, after her move, that cousin passed unexpectedly. She too had displayed indicators of someone sexually abused in early childhood, probably another victim of the generational curse in the family. Other older female cousins also were positive role models to Pam whenever their parents would brag on how well they did in school. This helped encourage her to stay focused on her studies so she too would get bragged on by the adults.

At school, a number of special teachers left a positive impact on Pam. During her elementary years she recalls her first grade teacher Martha Holmes, her fourth grade teacher Edna Collins, and her sixth grade teacher Jane Layman making special efforts to assist her with her struggles and leaving a positive impact on her throughout her academic career. Also in elementary school, she was a member of the Brownies. Her den mother Helen Burton and her daughter Cheryl also befriended Pam and left positive influences on her. Orgeron appreciates the friendship she had with the Burtons while in the Brownies and in later years.

In junior and senior high school, special teachers included the late Carl Thompson and Charles Chris. Carl was like family, as he was the brother to her mother's brother's wife. Mr. Chris was a devout Christian who genuinely cared about all the students. She had him for a number of courses, as he taught math and many of the science courses.

As for Pam's peers growing up, her closest girlfriends were the girls she went to church with. They know who they are, and Orgeron hopes they realize how much they meant being there through many difficult times while they were growing up. As for male friends, in high school Pam felt that she had more of those than she did female friends because she took mostly math and science courses, the college prep courses with them. Four special male friends from high school come to mind: Charles Justice, the late Harry "Buddy" McNurlin, Bart Norris, and David Sparks. Another connection that made them all feel special was that they all had fathers who were friends and/or worked with Pam's father. Orgeron remembers her friendship with Charles, Bart, and Buddy also carried over to junior college, as they all attended Ashland Community College following high school.

What can Orgeron say about Charles? He was funny and made everyone laugh. He also used to give Pam rides to Ashland Community College sometimes. She recalls one memorable experience riding with him. It was winter and the roads were icy. He was driving a jeep and Pam believes as a joke trying to scare her, he drove the jeep too fast and skidded with the jeep ending up in the ditch facing the opposite direction that they were headed.

Bart and Pam have their own story. Because teachers back then always sat students in alphabetical order and they both were the only ones with last names beginning with N and O, respectively, they were typically sat next to each other in their classes. A special memory of Bart is how he enabled her to go on their senior trip. When he heard that Pam's father was not going to allow her to go on the senior trip to Daytona Beach because of the reputations about what happens on senior trips, Bart promised Pam's father that he would look out for her, and he did too. She recalls when they and other classmates were at Boardwalk, a man high on drugs was trying to hit on Pam talking to her and getting closer to her. Scared, Pam practically jumped into Bart's lap who was sitting on a nearby bench. When Bart realized what was happening with the stranger, he gave him a dirty look like he dared him to bother Pam again. Their teacher Charles Chris, one of the chaperones for the trip, witnessed the whole incident and teased Pam later. She recalls him laughing and saying, "I didn't know you could move so fast." (Referring to how quickly Pam jumped to sit on the bench by Bart).

One memory of the late Buddy McNurlin stands out in Pam's mind. She remembers at a class Christmas party when she had taken homemade peanut butter balls for everyone to eat. Buddy really liked the candy, telling her, "With a woman who cooks like this, I think I'll marry you." At the time Pam did not acknowledge the comment in any way but now believes his remark subconsciously gave her hope that someday she would meet someone who would want to marry her. Her mother had told her that no man would ever have her because men didn't like "chubby" women.

Like Charles, David Sparks was another class clown keeping others laughing. Additionally, he and Pam served on the high school yearbook staff together. As seniors they were co-editors of the yearbook. She remembers the first time she met David was when both were in the 6th grade competing against each other in a regional spelling bee for their school district. Another girl a year ahead of them won the spelling bee.

Orgeron saved the topic of resilience for last to highlight because she believes it was an interaction of all the other protective factors that led her to become a resilient person. What is resilience? Simply stated, she defines resilience as the ability of a person to bounce back to what is considered normal or functional behavior after facing a crisis or trauma. Typically a resilient person easily constructs a positive meaning in the wake of a traumatic event.

To conclude this chapter, Orgeron would like to encourage those reading this book to speak positive words of encouragement to others. For those who are parents, teach children to compliment, not bully, their classmates. Who knows what a positive impact one could be leaving on a hurting soul by doing so?

***

Pamela K. Orgeron, M.A., Ed.S., BCCC, ACLC, BCMMHC

CHAPTER 9

Nehemiah . . . A Biblical Basis for Recovery

Author's Note: A large portion of this article has been extracted, updated, and edited from a blog written by the author. The blog was written January 15, 2018 entitled "'Sexual Abuse & Witnessing a Murder . . . It only happens in the movies. Wrong! It happened to me". The information in the blog regarding Nehemiah was initially shared by Pam in a personal testimony entitled "Removing the Debris" given in 2004 at a church where she spoke during the service which was followed by a book signing of her first book.

Recovery from any type of past abuse is similar to the grieving process depicted by Nehemiah. In Nehemiah 1:4, Nehemiah began his journey with weeping, mourning, fasting, and prayer, all key elements in the recovery process. Nehemiah 1:6 reveals how Nehemiah continued his journey with repentance for his sins and those of his people. Repentance involves breaking through denial, which many individuals prefer to live in after being abused. Before anyone can move on from being a victim of abuse, the damage from that abuse must be surveyed as Nehemiah went from gate to gate viewing the devastation of the temple walls. This scene is depicted in Nehemiah 2:13-15. On any road to healing, you can *expect opposition* just as Nehemiah (v. 2: 10, 19; vs. 4:1-3; vs.

6:1-14) faced opposition on his journey that included a conspiracy to assassinate him outlined in chapter 6.

Nehemiah **responded to opposition** with four things. First, Nehemiah turned to **prayer** for deliverance when faced with opposition. Secondly, we read in chapter 2, verses 16-18 that Nehemiah **called for help and unity** among the Jews. Thirdly, chapter 4, verses 16-18 reveals that Nehemiah and the Jews building the wall **kept watch for their enemies** and were always ready for battle. Lastly, Nehemiah and the others helping **persisted in working to complete the** task. Scripture reveals this in Nehemiah 6:15-19.

With Nehemiah the scriptural basis for needing to ponder the effects of abuse, how can others apply Nehemiah's journey to their recovery process? Orgeron offers a few suggestions that help with the *recounting process*. Among these suggestions are *journaling*, *psychotherapy* with a professional counselor, and *talking to a supportive group* of friends.

Complete recovery of "removing the debris" left by abuse requires a connection with and release of one's emotions. Recall how Nehemiah wept over the devastation. How can one find release from one's emotions? First, Pam found emotional connection and release through journaling. Journaling helped her discover her feelings and unlock repressed memories. Journaling also helped and still helps her keep track of her progress through recovery.

> **"Complete recovery of 'removing the debris' left by abuse requires a connection with and release of one's emotions."**

Emotional connection and release can be found through psychotherapy but remember different therapists have different styles. It's important to find a qualified therapist that one is comfortable with, preferably one who incorporates Christian ideology and techniques.

Emotional connection and release can be found through the help of a support group. Recall how Nehemiah recruited and organized other Jews to help him complete the building of the wall. Pam's primary support group became and still remains her church family. Other support groups include the numerous 12-step groups, such as Celebrate Recovery, Codependents Anonymous, Overeater's Anonymous, and many others.

Before a person sets out to rebuild a life that was damaged by abuse, the losses and damages to that life must be surveyed. Recall how Nehemiah surveyed the damage before rebuilding. Abuse can result in a variety of losses and negative effects. Losses from abuse can come in the form of missed opportunities. Orgeron thinks of how her perpetrators stole any chance for her to have a "normal" life.

Negative effects may be cognitive in nature. For example, sometimes going through depression Pam experienced problems concentrating.

Negative effects may include stress-related physical illnesses. Pam has had problems with TMJ, gastro esophageal reflux, nervous bladder, and other similar health issues.

Abuse damages one's emotions. For example, Pam often felt that she could never be good enough. These feelings drove her to strive for perfection, rather than progress. Though the Scriptures encourage Christians to "be perfect" (Matthew 5:48), most biblical scholars Orgeron has heard equate the biblical meaning of "perfect" to be maturity in Christ, rather than having to be right all the time in everything one does.

Relationship problems also occur as a result of abuse. The lack of trust created during abuse is a key factor here.

The "surveying" process should include education. A person who has experienced abuse needs to be continually educated on his or her particular issues. Education can come from reading books and articles, viewing documentaries, and tapping available community resources (for example, support groups and specialized counselors).

A quick "forgive and forget" mode encouraged by some does not lead to ultimate peace. The injury and its consequences must be acknowledged. Offering forgiveness does not condone the actions of the offender. Forgiveness acknowledges the complete work of Christ's blood on the cross. Even with the help of a therapist, a support group, or any other recovery tool, relapses will happen.

> **"Before a person sets out to rebuild a life that was damaged by abuse, the losses and damages to that life must be surveyed."**

A person in recovery can expect to face opposition on the journey to wellness. Opposition can come in the form of family or friends embarrassed by the abuse. As mentioned previously in this book, when Pam first entered psychotherapy, family members begged her to not look back. However, she knew she had to find peace and the answers she sought. After the memories returned and Pam confronted relatives with what she knew, she was accused of lying and became the black sheep in the family.

Satan also will throw stumbling blocks on the road to recovery. I Peter 5: 8 tells us, "⁸ Be [a]sober, be [b]vigilant; [c]because your adversary the devil walks about like a roaring lion, seeking whom he may devour". Just as Nehemiah faced attacks of criticism and ridicule and even the attempted assassination plot Christians too can protect themselves from Satan's attacks. How? First, as instructed by Ephesians 6:11, put on the whole armor of God. The Christian's spiritual weapons of defense based on

Ephesians 6 include truth, righteousness, the gospel of peace, faith, salvation, and the word of God. Additionally, as instructed in James 4:7, one should always seek to resist the devil. People should never compromise their convictions and try to deal with the devil. Note how in Nehemiah 6, Nehemiah held fast and refused to give in to the enemy's tricks.

Orgeron can't stress enough that when a person has been victimized or experienced loss similar to Nehemiah, he or she must recount the experience and survey its effects before offering forgiveness and moving on with one's life. Remember only the truth can set one free!

***

CHAPTER 10

Overcoming Through Therapy, Coaching, and Support Groups

Therapy, coaching and support groups are major tools individuals may use to overcome negative effects of trauma. In this chapter Orgeron first discusses a few of the major types of therapy and how therapy helped her. That discussion is followed by a brief introduction to coaching. Lastly, she discusses the value of support groups and how she found value in one particular support group, Celebrate Recovery

A vital member of the treatment team for a person facing the effects of generational or individual sin can be a psychologist. Treatment procedures of a therapist reflect his or her treatment philosophy. In treating victims who have experienced trauma psychologists often need to fill the role of educator as well as help the client deal with the broader problems that resulted from the trauma.

Before highlighting how Pam benefited from therapy and how she borrows therapy techniques in her ministry now, she will discuss key approaches to therapy. One popular form of therapy is cognitive-behavioral. Cognitive-behaviorists presume the primary vehicle for permanent recovery is cognitive; although, they assume lasting change occurs at many levels, including behavioral, cognitive, and emotional. The goal of cognitive-behavioral therapists is to have clients change unhealthy dysfunctional desires and behaviors into healthier more productive desires and behaviors through using techniques, such as giving homework assignments.

Cognitive techniques. Ridding the patient of self-defeating attitudes and beliefs surrounding the trauma is the goal of cognitive therapists. Old beliefs and attitudes are replaced with realistic, healthy ones.

Behavioral therapy. Many hospital and day programs incorporate behavior therapy into their programs. This approach is tailored to the needs of each client individually and focuses on eliminating old dysfunctional behavior to learn new healthier behavior patterns.

Many other therapy models exist but Orgeron only wishes to mention two others that she had therapists utilize with her in treatment. One is the psychodynamic model, which focuses on early experiences that may have contributed to current symptoms. The second approach is Gestalt therapy. One technique from Gestalt therapy that Pam experienced as a client and also uses as a Christian counselor is the "empty chair" technique, where an empty chair is placed in the room across from the client. The client is then asked to have an imaginary conversation with a perpetrator or someone of significance, such as Jesus Christ, in the person's life.

In her ministry, Orgeron considers herself a Christian eclectic counselor and life coach, meaning that she pulls and uses treatment techniques from the various treatment modalities, as long as the specific technique does not suggest doing anything contrary to Scripture.

What about coaching? Where does that fit in to overcoming generational curses and trauma? Orgeron does not believe that coaching can really get to the root of a client's problems resulting from generational sins or trauma because coaching does not delve deep into the past to find the origin of symptoms. However, what coaching can do is assist a client in learning new behaviors to move forward to reach goals established by the client.

To distinguish whether one wants therapy or coaching, Orgeron uses a common scenario. Suppose a person comes to her saying that he or she wants to lose weight. If the person requests counseling, she will ask the individual to look into the past to discover the root, when and how did overeating first become a problem. For instance, are the client's parents and grandparents overweight having a problem with overeating (generational sin)? If so, the root is probably learned sinful behavior that needs to be repented of and new healthier lifestyle behaviors adopted.

When a client wanting to lose weight does not want to look into the past, coaching is appropriate. With coaching, Orgeron helps the client find a healthy eating and exercise plan that will help the client reach his or her weight loss goal. In simpler terms, coaching focuses on the future rather than looking back.

Having both formal and informal support groups are important throughout recovery. Orgeron considers formal support groups as the numerous 12-step groups, such as Alcoholics Anonymous, Overeaters Anonymous, etc. One's Sunday school or another church group might also be considered a formal support group. An example of an Informal support group would be a group of friends meeting together somewhere to chat.

The formal support group that Orgeron has the most experience and knowledge about is Celebrate Recovery. God first led her to Celebrate Recovery in 2014. What's different about CR from past support groups? Orgeron uses the acronym **FAITH** to explain: "F" is for *F*riendships. She found more authentic and deeper friendships. "A" stands for *A*cceptance: self-acceptance, acceptance of others' differences, and a feeling of being accepted by others. "I" is for *I*ntimacy: intimacy with God and with others. The "T" represents *T*rust and *T*ruth: Orgeron's trust in God and in others has grown by leaps and bounds through relationships developed in CR. The truth: yes, it was tragic that her childhood was stolen from her as she was raped at the tender age of three years old, witnessed an attempted rape and murder at the age of four years old, and suffered from the effects of growing up in a family with mental illness. However, through her sponsor and through the testimonies of others at CR God has led her to realize that her childhood could have been worse. Through Christ she released the jealousy and resentment towards her brother for how their parents raised them with the double standard. Orgeron has a deeper realization that her parents' overprotectiveness of her and their being harder on her was out of love. The pain is gone. A greater appreciation for her parents' sacrifices and a deeper respect for her parents, herself and others who are different from her now reside in her heart.

The "H" in **FAITH** represents a deeper *h*ealing and a greater *h*ope for the future. Over the years Orgeron's CR forever family has helped her through the deaths of both her parents and through the realization in 2017 that her maternal grandfather was not only a pedophile but a murderer. Yes, one would have to say that CR has definitely taken Orgeron to deeper levels of healing. Just as God used CR to bring Orgeron to heal from her past trauma, she encourages others facing trauma to give such a group a chance to do the same for them.

***

CHAPTER 11

Education...a Door to Recovery

Both formal and self-taught education is probably two of the biggest tools in learning how to live with and overcome the consequences of generational curses. Throughout the healing process, an individual who has experienced for example early childhood sexual abuse should be continually educated on his or her problem issues.

Though formal education had many benefits for Pam, it came with many challenges. In the next several paragraphs she will highlight a few of those challenges through her academic years.

Problems that Orgeron attributes to Complex PTSD showed up quickly once she started school. First of all, she struggled paying attention in class. Her first grade teacher wrote home to her parents in a report card that she was a "daydreamer" and just stared out the window. Looking back, Orgeron thinks that was her dissociating. Well, that problem was overcome by her having to always sit right up front under the teacher's nose. She had no choice but to listen. She soon learned that listening got her good grades, and good grades got her positive attention, which she craved immensely. That also was when her parents adopted the "homework first" policy where when she got home from school, the first thing she had to do was her homework before she could do anything else. She became a straight "A" student. She also became very good at people pleasing (codependent), back then teased as being "teacher's pet" and a "brown noser".

A second problem Pam had in early elementary school, not related to school, was that she kept wetting the bed, a common symptom of children who experience abuse. She remembers being taken to a doctor to see if something was wrong. When the doctor found nothing wrong, he told her parents not to let her have anything to drink after dinner. Eventually, she outgrew that problem.

Pam continued to be a "star" student all through elementary school and got along well with all her teachers. Her relationship with many of her classmates was another matter. As mentioned previously, she was made fun of a lot for being a "teacher's pet". She also was made fun of because of the clothes she had to wear to school. When time came to buy school clothes, she was always bought dresses that doubled as church attire, and since her parents' church didn't believe in women wearing pants or shorts, she stood out appearance-wise from the other girls in her class who were allowed to wear pants and shorts. She also started putting on more weight than she should have, which gave her another nickname, "chubby". She also felt left out among her circle of friends at church, as she was the youngest in the crowd.

On the surface, Pam appeared to not be bothered by feeling left out from classmates and other children at church but deep down she was hurting. Thankfully, what got her through was her paternal grandmother Mama Owens, praise from being a "star" student, and God. Orgeron loved God so much. She remembers being at Mama's once when her grandmother asked her what she wanted to be when she grew up. She told Mama, "a writer, an author, because that way I could tell more people about Jesus."

Mama replied, "That's a ministry."

"What's that?" Pam asked her grandmother. Her grandmother explained the best she could for the young age of her granddaughter.

In junior high school Orgeron remembers all the students from the three elementary schools in her school district were assigned to three groups based on how well each student had done in elementary school. In the seventh grade, she was placed in group one but when she was upset not being able to compete with students from the other elementary schools and make straight A's like she had to have to be happy, she was moved down to group two in eighth grade where she became one of the top students in group two. She was known as the student who always blew the curve. Thus, she never felt like she fit in during junior high school either.

In high school Pam was popular, but only for her academic accomplishments. She had a few close friends at school but deep down she really felt like she didn't fit in with her classmates or with her family until she was about 16 years of age. At 16 years old, Pam made her first public profession of faith, joined the school's prayer group, and was slowly building more and better friendships. She took all the college prep courses, as much math and science as she could get. Because of her intelligence, her high school counselor and teachers told her she needed to go to college, and to take as much math and science as she could get. Trying to please everyone, including her father who wanted her to be a doctor, she complied, graduating as co-salutatorian and as the most outstanding math and science student in her class.

In undergraduate school Pam got a rude awakening. She jumped from high school trigonometry and algebra straight into college calculus. When she flunked her first calculus test she was crushed. She wasn't a quitter (obsessive-compulsive) so she went and signed up for a tutor, determined to finish the course. When she barely scraped through the class with a "D", she decided being a math teacher would not be a part of her future. She had always loved to write, and switched her major to English. No longer being the "star" student in her undergraduate courses was difficult and embarrassing for her at first. That was one way God humbled her to bring her back in line with what He wanted her to do in life, Christian ministry, in the form of writing, teaching, and counseling. Pam ended up graduating with her undergraduate degree in Journalism-Public Relations, with minors in English, psychology, and political science.

Graduate school...not in Pam's dreams! After taking 7.5 years to complete her bachelor's degree, she was glad to be out of school and thought all her test-taking was over. Boy was she wrong! In between graduating from undergraduate school and entering graduate school, God had a lot more humbling to do in Pam before she would make that decision. Humbling experiences included crushing her left ankle, Mama's death, a bout with depression and anxiety, and realizing she had been a victim of abuse. During that time she was misdiagnosed more than once. She remembers one psychiatrist who put her on medication for bipolar disorder. She started hallucinating and spacing out on the medication. Her psychologist noticed something was wrong on their next visit, and told her that she was not bipolar and to quit taking the medication immediately. Those are days Orgeron would not want to relive.

Pam's decision to attend graduate school came after getting through all the aforementioned crises and after she surrendered to a call to full-time vocational ministry. After surrendering to her calling, a former pastor advised her to try to go back to school to better prepare her for ministry. After praying for God's will, He opened the doors to make that possible. Looking back she is thankful for the obsessive-compulsive tendencies from the Complex PTSD that got her through graduate school making mostly A's.

Pam did have another challenge, a very humbling experience in graduate school. After being out of undergraduate school for about 10 years, she went straight into graduate statistics completely unprepared. She flunked the first test. Much wiser after her experience with calculus knowing how much the "D" had lowered her GPA, rather than get a tutor, she dropped the class immediately and went back to take undergraduate statistics 101 to refresh her math skills. She doesn't regret that decision even though it took her longer to complete her higher level degrees. She worked hard four long years to complete the two-year master's level degree, and another year or two to complete the Education Specialist degree.

In addition to formal education, Pam also taught herself a lot through reading self-help books and watching documentaries. She has developed a deep-seated love for learning and has committed to being a life-long learner. She encourages others, even if not in recovery, to do likewise.

***

Pamela K. Orgeron, M.A., Ed.S., BCCC, ACLC, BCMMHC

CHAPTER 12

Healing Through Prayer

Author's Note: This chapter is an updated and edited version of the book chapter entitled "Prayer, A Conversation with God" (pp. 85-89) in *Freedom in Truth*.

When Pam's paternal grandmother first started teaching her about prayer, she told her, "You can pray to God about anything just like you would tell a friend something. You can tell Him things you wouldn't want anyone else to know, and you don't have to worry about Him gossiping."

Over her lifetime Pam has learned several biblical principles about prayer. Among them are:

- People should pray about everything. Yes, that includes what one eats, what one wears, where one works, and whom one marries. At least, that's what the author encourages others to do. (Philippians 4:6)
- People need to believe God will answer a prayer when they pray. (Mark 11:24)
- Christians especially should always be in the frame of mind to pray. (1 Thessalonians 5:17; Luke 18:1)
- People need to pray through the power of the Holy Spirit, not in the flesh. (Romans 8:26; Ephesians 6:18)
- People need to pray in accordance with God's will. (1 John 5:14-15)

- People need to pray for their family, friends, political leaders, everybody! (1 Timothy 2:1-4) And, yes, that includes one's enemies too! (Matthew 5:44)
- Prayer is a way to avoid and resist temptation. (Matthew 26:41)
- Prayer combined with fasting is a tool to cast out demons. (Matthew 17:21; Mark 9:29)

One can find a number of theologians and other authors who share different prayer principles; these are the ones that work for the author.

Years ago Pam learned an acronym for how to pray, which is a good model for anyone to use: **ACTS**:

- A—A stands for **A**doration. This is where a person approaches God with the utmost love and respect for Him.
- C—C stands for **C**onfession. This is where people confess their sins and shortcomings to God asking Him to forgive them where they fail Him.
- T—T stands for **T**hanksgiving. This is where people thank God for Who He is and how He has provided for them.
- S—S stands for **S**upplication. This is where someone asks God to meet the needs of others or one's own self.

When one of Jesus' disciples asked Him to teach them how to pray, He responded with the following prayer:

"9 In this manner, therefore, pray:

Our Father in heaven,
Hallowed be Your name.
10 Your kingdom come.
Your will be done
On earth as it is in heaven.
11 Give us this day our daily bread.
12 And forgive us our debts,
As we forgive our debtors.

> *¹³ And do not lead us into temptation,*
> *But deliver us from the evil one.*
> *For Yours is the kingdom and the power and the glory forever. Amen" (Matthew 6:9-13, NKJV).*

Additionally, Pam has learned over the years that the more she prays the easier praying gets. When she faces a decision to make or is facing an obstacle, praying has almost always become her nature to do immediately without whining or complaining first. Sometimes, she finds herself praying without thinking about it. For example, when she is out in public somewhere and sees a handicapped individual, the Holy Spirit often prompts her to pray immediately for the needs of that individual and to pray a prayer of thanksgiving thanking Him for her many blessings. That's how God works.

As Orgeron mentioned previously prayer is a conversation with God, a two-way street, not just an individual always talking to Him. For prayer to be an effective prayer, one must learn to listen to God too. One common definition to listen means to obey. What does God's Word say about listening and obeying God?

> *⁴⁷ Whoever comes to Me, and hears My sayings and does them, I will show you whom he is like: ⁴⁸ He is like a man building a house, who dug deep and laid the foundation on the rock. And when the flood arose, the stream beat vehemently against that house, and could not shake it, for it was founded on the rock. ⁴⁹ But he who heard and did nothing is like a man who built a house on the earth without a foundation, against which the stream beat vehemently; and immediately it fell. And the ruin of that house was great" (Luke 6:47-49, NKJV).*

How does God speak to a person? There are five possible ways:
- Through the Scripture

- Through circumstances
- Through other Christian people
- Through dreams
- Through the still small voice of the Holy Spirit.

Based on the discussion thus far about prayer and the author's interpretations of what God's Word says about prayer, let's look closer at how prayer helped Pam during her physical abuse, following the trauma of the attempted rape/murder that she witnessed, and during her recovery from all the abuse and trauma. During the times that Pam was being physically abused, prayer gave her the strength and patience to take what was being dished out. She could have fought back, which, no doubt, would have made matters much worse.

> "...prayer is a conversation with God, a two-way street, not just an individual always talking to Him. For prayer to be an effective prayer, one must learn to listen to God too."

Following the rape/murder scam that others tried to deny and cover up, the Lord spoke to Pam through her paternal grandmother to stand for the truth, and not back down. Looking back, in one way she is proud of the way she handled myself at the time of the attempted rape and murder to have been so young. No doubt, the Holy Spirit was with her guiding her steps. Yet another part of Orgeron wishes she could have done more, wishes she could have saved the victim's life. Then she gets sad, as the Holy Spirit reminds her that God had a purpose in allowing the victim to die—a far greater purpose that she might not fully understand this side of Heaven.

During Pam's recovery, how did prayer help her? Well, to be honest, without prayer, she believes that she would have never recovered. Without her prayer for God to reveal to her what was wrong with her and what had happened to cause her to have such a low self-esteem and fail so miserably at life, or so Satan had her believing, she might not have ever remembered what happened and could have lived a miserable life taking all those secrets to her grave like others in her family chose to do. No doubt, the author's remembering as many details as she remembers surrounding the tragedies of her preschool years was a gift of revelation from God.

Throughout Pam's recovery days, she has always prayed for God to take her to deeper levels of healing. To go to deeper levels of healing God used her doctors, pastors, other victims, and all of the people and experiences associated with her post-undergraduate work. For Pam returning to college for graduate work killed two birds with one stone, as the old saying goes. First, she applied the facts she learned in the classroom to her story, which brought further healing. Secondly, both her formal education and her informal self-learning through reading, watching documentaries, etc. have prepared her to identify with and encourage other victims who have experienced similar circumstances, which is one of the motives behind writing this book. This motive is scripturally motivated:

"[3] Blessed be the God and Father of our Lord Jesus Christ, the Father of mercies and God of all comfort, [4] who comforts us in all our tribulation, that we may be able to comfort those who are in any trouble, with the comfort with which we ourselves are comforted by God. [5] For as the sufferings of Christ abound in us, so our consolation also abounds through Christ" (2 Corinthians 1:3-5, NKJV).

For Orgeron, prayer is the foundation and most important part of her having a personal daily relationship with God. She can go to God in prayer anytime, anywhere, with any concern. He may not always answer her immediately or in the way she expects but she believes He always knows best. Orgeron also believes that there are three primary ways God will answer prayers. These ways are "yes," "no," or "wait".

To conclude this chapter, the author wants to point out that the most important prayer/decision anyone can ever make is the sinner's prayer. For those who have not prayed that prayer, she shares The ABC's of Salvation (Orgeron, *Why Didn't They Hear Us*, p. 95):

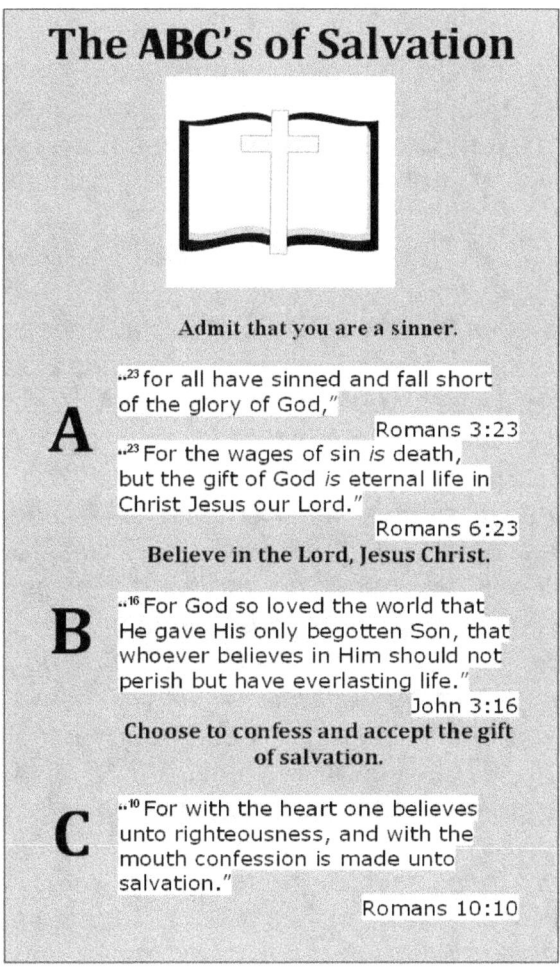

***

Pamela K. Orgeron, M.A., Ed.S., BCCC, ACLC, BCMMHC

CHAPTER 13

Healing Through Scripture

Pam found much healing through the Scriptures and encourages others in recovery to look to the Bible for healing. To exemplify how the Scriptures have helped Pam in recovery, she shares an excerpt from a journal entry:

6:30 p.m., May 24, 1991

...I guess I'll get into my self-talk assignment now.
Let's first research what the Scripture says about death. What verses could be or could have been used to comfort me when faced with the loss of a loved one through death? Jesus would tell me that it's okay to be sad and cry when someone dies. He'd also tell me death was a natural part of life—I base this on Ecclesiastes 3:1-8. Verses 1-2 (NKJV) state "To everything there is a season, A time for every purpose under heaven: ²A time to be born, And a time to die; A time to plant, And a time to pluck what is planted;" Verse 4 (NKJV) says "A time to weep, And a time to laugh; A time to mourn, And a time to dance;". The verse Romans 12:15 (NKJV) says "Rejoice with those who rejoice, and weep with those who weep." (NKJV) Matthew 5:4 (NKJV) says "Blessed are those who mourn, For they shall be comforted."
While I'm in the Scriptures, let me jot down a verse my grandmother used to quote to me all the time whenever I complained about something wrong. She said to expect

trouble in this world. She quoted Job 14:1 (KJV): "Man that is born of a woman is of few days and full of trouble." Maybe besides my mother's negative attitudes and all, this statement of my grandmother's helped to contribute to my always expecting the worst. Oh, well, we'll overcome all this.

What would Jesus have said about the fear I had when I thought my father would leave me like my cousin's father did? For this, I use Psalms 27:10 (NKJV)—"When my father and my mother forsake me, Then the LORD will take care of me."; and Proverbs 18:24 (NKJV)—"A man who has friends must himself be friendly, But there is a friend who sticks closer than a brother." Jesus would tell me that my Heavenly Father will always be with me to take care of me.

Now let's look for some Scriptures I can use to become an overcomer—and I do intend to be an overcomer in Christ.

What are the Scriptures that Pam found over 30 years ago that she has pulled from over the years as needed to help her in overcoming generational curses? They are (all NKJV):

> "But those who wait on the LORD
> Shall renew their strength;
> They shall mount up with wings like eagles,
> They shall run and not be weary,
> They shall walk and not faint" (Isaiah 40: 31).

***

> "casting all your care upon Him, for He cares for you"
> (1 Peter 5:7).

Pamela K. Orgeron, M.A., Ed.S., BCCC, ACLC, BCMMHC

"But without faith *it is* impossible to please *Him,* for he who comes to God must believe that He is, and *that* He is a rewarder of those who diligently seek Him" (Hebrews 11:6).

***

"'Call to Me, and I will answer you, and show you great and mighty things, which you do not know'" (Jeremiah 33:3).

***

"Commit your way to the LORD,
Trust also in Him,
And He shall bring it to pass" (Psalm 37:5).

***

"In all your ways acknowledge Him,
And He shall direct your paths" (Proverbs 3:6).

***

Draw near to God and He will draw near to you. Cleanse *your* hands, *you* sinners; and purify *your* hearts, *you* double-minded (James 4:8).

***

"The LORD will perfect that which concerns me;
Your mercy, O LORD, endures forever;
Do not forsake the works of Your hands" (Psalm 138:8).
"And whatever things you ask in prayer, believing, you will receive" (Matthew 21:22).

"Ask, and it will be given to you; seek, and you will find; knock, and it will be opened to you" (Matthew 7:7).

***

*"Cast your burden on the L*ORD*,
And He shall sustain you;
He shall never permit the righteous to be moved"
(Psalm 55:22).*

***

*"A faithful man will abound with blessings…"
(Proverbs 28:20).*

***

"Humble yourselves in the sight of the Lord, and He will lift you up" (James 4:10).

***

*"Call upon Me in the day of trouble;
I will deliver you, and you shall glorify Me" (Psalm 50:15).*

***

*"Though I walk in the midst of trouble, You will revive me;
You will stretch out Your hand
Against the wrath of my enemies,
And Your right hand will save me" (Psalm 138:7).*

***

Pamela K. Orgeron, M.A., Ed.S., BCCC, ACLC, BCMMHC

*"Call upon Me in the day of trouble;
I will deliver you, and you shall glorify Me" (Psalm 50:15).*

***

*"Come to Me, all you who labor and are heavy laden,
and I will give you rest" (Matthew 11:28).*

***

*"My help comes from the LORD,
Who made heaven and earth" (Psalm 121:2).*

***

*"God is our refuge and strength,
A very present help in trouble" (Psalm 46:1).*

***

*"The righteous cry out, and the LORD hears,
And delivers them out of all their troubles" (Psalm 34:17).
"He gives power to the weak,
And to those who have no might He increases strength"
(Isaiah 40:29).*

***

*"He heals the brokenhearted,
And binds up their wounds" (Psalm 147:3).*

***

Overcoming Generational Curses

*"Many are the afflictions of the righteous,
But the LORD delivers him out of them all"* (Psalm 34:19).

***

*"The LORD also will be a refuge for the oppressed,
A refuge in times of trouble"* (Psalm 9:9).

***

"Again I say to you that if two of you agree on earth concerning anything that they ask, it will be done for them by My Father in heaven" (Matthew 18:19).

***

"If you ask anything in My name, I will do it" (John 14:14).

***

"For with God nothing will be impossible" (Luke 1:37).

***

"…as I was with Moses, so I will be with you" (Joshua 3:7)

***

*"The LORD is my strength and song,
And He has become my salvation;
He is my God, and I will praise Him;
My father's God, and I will exalt Him"* (Exodus 15:2).

Pamela K. Orgeron, M.A., Ed.S., BCCC, ACLC, BCMMHC

"Fear not, for I am with you;
Be not dismayed, for I am your God.
I will strengthen you, Yes, I will help you,
I will uphold you with My righteous right hand.'"
(Isaiah 41:10).

***

"And He said, 'My Presence will go with you, and I will give you rest'" (Exodus 33:14).

***

"Yea, though I walk through the valley
of the shadow of death, I will fear no evil;
For You are with me;
Your rod and Your staff, they comfort me" (Psalm 23:4).

***

"Have I not commanded you? Be strong and of good courage; do not be afraid, nor be dismayed, for the L ORD *your God is with you wherever you go"*
(Joshua 1:9).

***

"…God is with you in all that you do" (Genesis 21:22).

***

"then the Lord knows how to deliver the godly out of temptations and to reserve the unjust under punishment for the day of judgment," (2 Peter 2:9)).

"…Forgive, and you will be forgiven" (Luke 6:37).

***

*"For the LORD God is a sun and shield;
The LORD will give grace and glory;
No good thing will He withhold
From those who walk uprightly" (Psalm 84:11).*

***

*"Delight yourself also in the LORD,
And He shall give you the desires of your heart"
(Psalm 37:4).*

***

"And He said to me, 'My grace is sufficient for you, for My strength is made perfect in weakness.' Therefore most gladly I will rather boast in my infirmities, that the power of Christ may rest upon me" (2 Corinthians 12:9).).

***

"He who overcomes shall inherit all things, and I will be his God and he shall be My son" (Revelation 21:7).

***

"And we know that all things work together for good to those who love God, to those who are the called according to His purpose" (Romans 8:28).

Pamela K. Orgeron, M.A., Ed.S., BCCC, ACLC, BCMMHC

"He who overcomes, I will make him a pillar in the temple of My God…" (Revelation 3:12).

***

"I will instruct you and teach you in the way you should go; I will guide you with My eye" (Psalm 32:8).

***

*"You will show me the path of life;
In Your presence is fullness of joy;
At Your right hand are pleasures forevermore"
(Psalm 16:11).*

***

"And my God shall supply all your need according to His riches in glory by Christ Jesus" (Philippians 4:19).

***

*"Wait on the L*ORD*; Be of good courage,
And He shall strengthen your heart;
Wait, I say, on the L*ORD*!" (Psalm 27:14).).*

***

"The thief does not come except to steal, and to kill, and to destroy. I have come that they may have life, and that they may have it more abundantly" (John 10:10).

***

"Jesus Christ is the same yesterday, today, and forever" Hebrews 13:8).

***

"For I am the LORD, *I do not change..." (Malachi 3:6).*

Orgeron's prayer is that each person reading *Overcoming Generational Curses* will find strength, comfort, and encouragement from each of the Scriptures shared in this chapter. She encourages everyone to instill the Word of God in their hearts and minds through Bible Study and Scripture memorization.

***

Pamela K. Orgeron, M.A., Ed.S., BCCC, ACLC, BCMMHC

CHAPTER 14

Healing Through Writing and Other Creative Arts

Incorporating the creative arts into one's lifestyle is an excellent way to overcome and heal from the effects of generational and one's personal sins or poor choices. Creative arts could be considered writing, drawing, painting, woodworking, sewing, quilting, or any other creative endeavor that an individual enjoys doing; the primary tools of recovery among the creative arts for Pam have included writing, sewing Christmas crafts, and quilting.

Writing has so many diverse forms and ways of being used that to try to cover them all would be beyond the scope of this book. Thus, Orgeron will discuss how writing has played an important role in her life. She does not remember a time when she did not like to write.

In elementary school the author remembers one of her teachers while teaching about poetry used to encourage the students to write poems that would be placed on the bulletin board for everyone to read. Orgeron remembers at least one of her poems being hung on the board. She was very proud when that happened because only the best poems were selected from the entire class to be displayed. Also, in elementary school, a popular thing among her female classmates was to have diaries that they wrote in. After hearing her girlfriends talk about how they had and wrote in diaries, one Christmas Pam asked her parents to buy her a diary. She remembers the diary being her favorite present that year and how much it helped her to have a safe place to vent about all the dysfunction in her life at that time.

Writing in her diary did not last long though. Why? One day Pam's mother found her diary hidden in a drawer and broke into the diary to read the contents. Her mother, angered by what she read, threw all of her daughter's diaries in the garbage can without telling her. When Pam missed the diaries the next time she went to write, she remembers asking her mother if she knew where her diaries were. Her mother told her the diaries were in the garbage can where they belonged. She recalls her mother saying, "I'd be embarrassed to write and say the things you wrote about my parents. I wouldn't want people to know."

When Pam went to the garbage can to try to retrieve her dairies, she found them destroyed. Needless, to say she was very hurt and angry over her mother's actions. She never wrote another personal journal entry anywhere until her first therapist gave her journal writing as a homework assignment. She did do a lot of other formal and professional writing during that time gap though. She wrote a lot as co-editor of her high school yearbook. In undergraduate school, she wrote for two different school newspapers, both as a reporter and editor in chief. Additionally, for one semester she wrote for her undergraduate school's radio station as a student reporter for a class. During the time lapse, Pam also had a number of "Letters to the Editor" published in her hometown newspaper.

As an adult, Pam first broadened the scope of her writing to include song lyrics. Not a professional musician, she paid someone to create melodies to accompany her lyrics. Obviously a lot of writing of papers would be a part of her getting her post-graduate degrees. She also added to her writing experience the creation of a website that included a blog page. She has authored and published eight books.

Pamela K. Orgeron, M.A., Ed.S., BCCC, ACLC, BCMMHC

Pam's first book *The ABC's of Life for Children and Adults: Short Stories, Essays, and Poems Promoting Christian Concepts* (Xulon Press, 2003) was a compilation of manuscripts she had written to become certified as a writer with the Institute of Children's Literature (April 2000.).

When Orgeron's first attempt to start a Christian counseling business failed in 2015, she felt God's calling to start writing books because the Holy Spirit put it on her heart that she could reach more hurting people through books rather than having a private Christian counseling business. To teach herself about the process of self-publishing, she wrote an updated version to her first book. That book is *The New ABC's of Life for Children and Adults: Short Stories, Essays, and Poems Promoting Christian Concepts* (ABC's Ministries, 2016). After getting her feet wet in self-publishing with her second book, she followed that book with four self-help books: *We Survived Sexual Abuse! You Can Too!: Personal Stories of Sexual Abuse Survivors with Information about Sexual Abuse Prevention, Effects, and Recovery* (ABC's Ministries, 2016); *Food as an Idol: Finding Freedom from Disordered Eating* (ABC's Ministries, 2017); *Food as an Idol: The Types, Causes, Consequences, Conquering, and Prevention of Disordered Eating* (ABC's Ministries, 2019); and, *Why Didn't They Hear Us? The Causes, Consequences, and Solutions to Children Feeling Unheard* (Author Academy Elite, 2020). In 2021, *Why Didn't They Hear Us?* made the "Top 10 Finalist" list in the Author Elite Awards Self-Help Category.

In addition to the other books Orgeron self-published, Orgeron also self-published a biography, *A Legacy to Remember: "Recollections of a Common Man"* (ABC's Ministries, 2018). As Co-Author and Editor she shared the life story of her late cousin D. V. Gillum who experienced The Great Depression, divorced parents, living in poverty, World War II, the death of a child, divorce, etc.—commonly known occurrences many individuals in American History have faced. The biography stems out of Gillum's autobiography *Recollections of a Common Man* (Xlibris, 2011). In his autobiography, Gillum requested that a relative take his book and write the final chapter after his passing. The Lord opened the door seven years after Gillum's passing for Orgeron to edit, add a final chapter, and add more photos to what he had done in the autobiography. As close as Gillum was to her father and her, she would have felt remiss in not doing so.

Pam's love of sewing and making crafts no doubt comes from her paternal grandmother. She recalls her grandmother helping her make clothes for her Barbie dolls when she was a young child. She also took home economics in high school that broadened her sewing skills. The year she took home economics, her parents bought her a sewing machine for Christmas that she still has and uses to this day. She has used the sewing machine to mend and make clothing items, stuffed Christmas trees, ornaments, and other Christmas decorations. Some of her craft creations she sold at a number of craft fairs that she has participated in over the years.

Quilting was the last art that Orgeron taught herself to do. She had always watched her paternal grandmother make quilts when she was a little girl. However, her grandmother never had the chance to teach her so she went to the Internet and taught herself.

For Pam, the writing, sewing and other creative arts proved to be very therapeutic. Doing them has helped build her self-confidence and relieve stress. She encourages others to find a hobby or some form of creative expression to help them relieve stress and overcome past generational curses.

***

Pamela K. Orgeron, M.A., Ed.S., BCCC, ACLC, BCMMHC

CHAPTER 15

Forgiveness, Grieving the Losses, and Reparenting through Positive Self-Talk

In addition to educating oneself, praying, using Scripture, and the other tools advocated in this book to deal with the consequences of generational curses and sins, Orgeron suggests three processes are major keys to overcoming and living with the effects of generational curses. These processes are forgiveness of self and others, grieving the losses, and reparenting through positive self-talk.

Whether a person has been offended at another person or disappointed in a personal shortcoming, forgiveness is not optional. Christ said,

"For if you forgive men their trespasses, your heavenly Father will also forgive you. But if you do not forgive men their trespasses, neither will your Father forgive your trespasses" (Matthew 6:14-15, NKJV).

Years ago in early recovery Pam only thought of forgiveness in terms of the victim forgiving the person who offended. However, not only is forgiving others important; but, forgiving oneself for past mistakes and any damage done to self in reaction to a generational curse or sin is crucial to finding freedom at the Cross.

What is forgiveness? Forgiveness does not imply forgetting, does not condone the behavior, or let the person "off the hook". What victims need to remember is that God tells us, "... "Vengeance *is* Mine, I will repay..." (Romans 12:19, NKJV). By forgiving an offender, one is not saying that what the person did is okay but that he or she will not seek vengeance. God will take care of that: "Do not be deceived, God is not mocked; for **what**ever a man **sow**s, that he will also **reap**" (Galatians 6:7, NKJV).

Unforgiveness is a sin. Just as with lying, stealing, covetousness or any other sin, unforgiveness can leave a person in bondage. Not only a person, but entire families! For example, the author has heard of family feuds lasting for years where family members did not even know what started the feud. Somewhere along the line, two individuals had a problem. One, or maybe both persons, got mad. The anger became unforgiveness; the unforgiveness became bitterness. Then through the family grapevines the entire family of both parties became riled. How pleased is God when this happens?

Orgeron stresses the importance of victims realizing that forgiveness is a choice that can only be done through the power of the Holy Spirit living in an individual. Once the

> **"By forgiving an offender, one is not saying that what the person did is okay but that he or she will not seek vengeance."**

offended understands what encompasses forgiveness, can he or she offer forgiveness? Not yet! There's something else one must do first—grieve the losses. She knows from personal experience how vital forgiveness is in the life of any individual. However, many Christians, as was she, are encouraged to enter into a quick "forgive and forget" mode before working through their emotions and allowing healing of the heart. The losses and harm resulting from generational sins need to be acknowledged and grieved.

Orgeron thinks that for some people forgiveness may be a lifelong process due to the seriousness of the offense and triggers that remind the offended of what happened. Orgeron admits that though she has left the sins and consequences of her forefathers at the foot of the Cross, at times she needs to take them back to the Cross. Sometimes she will be triggered with memories of how atrocious her grandfather's or other perpetrators' actions were. If she dwells on the memories too long, she can find herself getting angry all over again. Is being angry at such atrocities a sin? After researching the Scriptures for what God says about anger, Orgeron found there is no sin in being angry. The sin begins when a person allows anger to fester into bitterness without forgiveness or when that person seeks to obtain vengeance or get back at the person or object of anger.

In early recovery Pam struggled with letting go of her anger. She wrote the following in one of her journals:

> *What hinders my letting go of anger to find complete healing? How can I overcome these hindrances? The number one cause of my hanging on to anger is fear. The fear is of a variety of dimensions: fear of the unknown, fear of rejection, fear of failure, etc. But it all boils down to one word: fear.*

Later in recovery, Pam learned that anger also can be a symptom of a different and sometimes deeper issue that may be masked by the anger. For example, anger is one of the five stages of grief (denial; anger; bargaining; depression; and, acceptance). Other root causes of anger at different times in Pam's life are anger as an indicator of unfinished business and anger rooted in an unforgiving heart.

On July 16, 2018 Orgeron wrote a blog article on her ABC's Ministries website entitled "No immunity to Anger". In the article, she developed what she referred to as "ABC's of Anger Management". The model was based on her belief that managing angry feelings effectively in a healthy way involves four primary paths: **A**djusting attitudes and thoughts; **B**uilding healthier behaviors; and, **C**ommunicating more constructively. Of course, the "**s**" represents spirituality, which she believes affects every aspect of every individual and is the most important means of dealing with angry feelings.

Once the losses are grieved and one is ready to offer forgiveness, how is this done? Is confronting the offender necessary? No, one need not communicate with the offender directly to offer forgiveness. In some instances, that would be impossible, for example, if the offender is deceased or his or her whereabouts unknown. Forgiveness does not equate to reconciliation. In some situations, a direct confrontation expecting reconciliation would only make matters worse leading to more pain in one or both parties. Thus, Orgeron suggests one way that she has been able to forgive past offenders. She wrote letters to the individuals, expressing how she felt offended and that she was choosing to forgive the wrongs against her. She does not recommend mailing such letters.

When damaged by the sins or mistakes of one's forefathers, one must learn the process of reparenting. What reparenting does is get rid of old negative false beliefs and thoughts learned from the offense to replace the thoughts with healthier thoughts that can result in a more mature, healthier self-esteem and behavior patterns. For example, in Orgeron's life, for decades she lived out a "self-fulfilling prophecy" that developed out of her mother's constantly telling her, "You'll never get married. No man would ever want to marry you. Men don't like chubby women." Hearing that statement coming from her mother so much as a young child and teenager Pam subconsciously accepted what was said as the truth. Thus, she would sabotage any relationship she got into staying single much longer than she had dreamed of in her early childhood. In hindsight, Orgeron can find good in her delaying marriage because she needed time on her own and away from dysfunctional environments where she could get stronger and learn healthier attitudes and behavior patterns to apply in her marriage now. Not that she or her marriage is perfect but as her husband Milton says, "God knew what He was doing bringing us together. Neither one of us is perfect but we are perfect for each other."

> **"What reparenting does is get rid of old negative false beliefs and thoughts learned from the offense to replace the thoughts with healthier thoughts that can result in a more mature, healthier self-esteem and behavior patterns."**

Reparenting can be done through positive self-affirmation. Positive self-affirmation was a major part of Pam's healing. What she loved to use for self-affirmation statements and still uses are Scriptures. For example, "I can do all things through Christ which strengtheneth me" (Philippians 4:13, NKJV).

***

Step Three: Moving Forward and Allowing God to Use You

Simple Ways to Serve

Cut Grass

Clean House

Cook a Meal

Help with Homework

CHAPTER 16

Remember Relapse Happens

Even with the help of a therapist, a support group, etc., relapses will happen. A person in recovery can expect to face opposition on the journey to wellness. For example, opposition can come in the form of family or friends embarrassed by the abuse, such as when Pam's family begged her to not look back. Such times of opposition may tempt a person to give up and lose any progress made in recovery, thus, creating relapse.

Stages of Relapse

Author's Note: The below section of this chapter has been extracted, updated, and edited from a blog written by the author. The blog was written May 20, 2018 entitled "'Disordered Eating Relapse Prevention".

Arterburn and Mintle (2004) discussed "the phases of relapse" [1]. These phases or stages include complacency, confusion, compromise, and catastrophe. In this book the author generalizes the stages, whether one is in recovery from disordered eating, an alcohol and drug problem or anything negative triggered by abuse and trauma.

Complacency. This is when those in recovery first let their guard down and neglect doing what they need to do, what they have been doing that has helped them move towards healing. During this stage people may think they no longer need help. Thus, they may relax their boundaries and even drop support groups or therapy that have been keys to their previous progress.

Confusion. Secondly, they become double-minded. Doubt is the dominant thought. They have doubts about the seriousness of the consequences of what happened or whether they need additional long-term treatment and support. Their recovery plan is put on the back burner with unhealthy and erratic choices made.

Compromise. During the phase of compromise, people revert to old patterns of thinking and acting. Because they refuse to accept responsibility for their actions and pull further away from their support team, they are headed for disaster.

Catastrophe. At this stage, those who have backslidden have lost any and all previous feelings of control. They are no longer making progress in recovery, often feeling helpless or without hope.

What can people in relapse do to get back on track? First, Orgeron recommends they get back into professional treatment as soon as possible. Additionally, they can reconnect with any support systems (e.g. 12-step groups) that they may have lost contact with. Those in relapse also need to reflect on what happened to bring on the relapse. What were the triggers? Once they recognize the triggers, avoid them.

Remember relapse does not make a person a failure. Experiencing relapse can make a person stronger. Orgeron firmly believes that a major key to overcoming relapse and in recovery in general is to make self-care a priority, striving for a permanent healthy lifestyle. She has told more than one client that self-care is not selfish. She learned that from her first therapist who used Scripture to support self-care.

"... 'You shall love your neighbor as yourself'" (Matthew 22:39, NKJV).

After sharing the above Scripture, her therapist asked her, "If you don't love and take care of yourself, how can you expect anyone else to love you?" That question from her therapist was a big eye-opener for Pam.

Orgeron's Remedy for Reducing Relapse

Orgeron encourages all people, whether a client, friend, or whomever, to practice self-care that will lead to ultimate wellness. Before diving into the topic of self-care that leads to ultimate wellness, how does Orgeron define wellness? As a researcher working on her thesis to receive her Education Specialist degree, she adopted the definition of wellness used by Myers and Sweeney [2, 3], developers of the wellness instrument that she used in her graduate research study, *Exploration Linking Self-Reported Disordered Eating and Wellness in Undergraduate Health Students* (Morehead State University, 2009). In her thesis written under her maiden name Owens, Orgeron considered

> **"...a major key to overcoming relapse and in recovery in general is to make self-care a priority, striving for a permanent healthy lifestyle. She has told more than one client that self-care is not selfish."**

> *"wellness as a way of life oriented toward optimal health and well-being in which body, mind, and spirit are integrated by the individual to live more fully within the human and natural community. Ideally, it is the optimum state of health and well-being that each individual is capable of achieving".* [4]

Let's look at what Pam gleaned from the above definition of wellness: She focused on three key points. First, consider the phrase "way of life". That told Pam there is permanency involved with having a lifestyle of wellness. Over the years she applied this to her personal desire to achieve and maintain a healthy weight. What she knows professionally and personally is that "fad diets" do not work. What works to achieve and maintain a healthy weight is adopting a permanent healthy lifestyle that includes a healthy diet, moderate exercise, and adequate sleep. Remember, though relapses will happen.

Besides eating healthily, getting moderate exercise and adequate sleep, what are other components of self-care? Orgeron believes other key ingredients of self-care that promote a lifestyle of wellness where one lives as healthy as possible for as long as possible are stress management, safe driving, choosing friends wisely, setting and maintaining healthy boundaries, and keeping God the first priority in life.

Orgeron's paternal grandmother had an old saying, "You can't choose the family that you were born into but you can sure choose your friends". Orgeron believes her grandmother was right. She also gleaned two truths from the statement that all victims need to understand. The first truth is that people have no choice as to the family that they are born into so they have no control over the generational curses passed on to them. What they do have control over is their reaction to the cards that they were dealt by being born into a particular family. They must make a conscience choice to break the generational chains to move towards ultimate well-being in life.

The second truth that Orgeron gleans from her grandmother's above comment is that the type of friends people choose can make or break them as a person. Everyone should consider their closest friends. Do they encourage and have a positive effect on them? Or do they pull them down, encouraging them to partake in unhealthy behaviors resulting in relapse?

> "[33] Do not be deceived: 'Evil company corrupts good habits.' [34] Awake to righteousness, and do not sin; for some do not have the knowledge of God… "
> (1 Corinthians 15:33-34, NKJV).

Orgeron believes that the Scriptures, the Word of God, should be the ultimate authority in making any decision that one has to make in life. Any decision that a victim in recovery from generational sin or even personal sins makes should be bathed in prayer with guidance sought through the Scriptures and wise Christian counsel. Doing so can reduce the risk of relapsing into unhealthy generational curses.

> *"[33] But seek first the kingdom of God and His righteousness, and all these things shall be added to you"*
> *(Matthew 6:33, NKJV).*

***

Notes

[1] Arterburn, S. & Mintle, L. (2004, 2011). *Lose it for life: The total solution—spiritual, emotional, physical—for permanent weight loss.* Nashville: Integrity, 228-230.

[2] Myers, J. E., & Sweeney, T. J. (Eds.). (2005a). Counseling for wellness: Theory, research, and practice. Alexandria, VA: American Counseling Association.

[3] Myers, J. E., & Sweeney, T. J. (2005b). Manual for the Five Factor Wellness Inventory (5F-Wel) Adult, Teenage, Elementary School Versions. Greensboro, NC: Author.

[4] Myers, J. E., Sweeney, T. J., & Witmer, J. M. (2000). The Wheel of Wellness Counseling for Wellness: A Holistic Model for Treatment Planning. Journal of Counseling and Development, 78(3), 252.

Pamela K. Orgeron, M.A., Ed.S., BCCC, ACLC, BCMMHC

CHAPTER 17

Stay Focused

Choosing recovery for yourself, and setting it as the foremost goal for your life, is progress in its own right, and something to be proud of. As you strive toward that goal, however, you will inevitably encounter obstacles along the way. The road to recovery is never perfectly smooth, and some days will be better than others. The question is, how do you stay focused on recovery even during hard times? [1]

Recovering from and staying committed to overcoming negative effects of generational curses takes a lot of effort and focus. Orgeron knows this truth from her own experience. In hindsight, she believes that due to the Holy Spirit being in her life, her recovery from breaking the generational curses in her family began long before she realized that she was a victim and before she first entered professional treatment after being diagnosed with depression, anxiety, and codependency in 1989. Why does she say that? She remembers at an early age noticing unhealthy behavior patterns in her family and making up her mind then that she would do differently. One such example involves how husbands and wives, and families should relate to each other.

In her earlier and even up into her teen years Orgeron remembers a lot of screaming and yelling occurring in their home. Witnessing that made her feel insecure and to think, *if this is what marriage is all about, I don't want anything to do with it.* Thus, she built an emotional wall around herself determined not to ever fall in love. However, that wall did not keep Pam from developing feelings for one of her best male friends in high school. In that relationship she learned that love can be a good thing. Furthermore, in her late teens and early 20s she began to be exposed to healthier families where arguing was not the norm in the home. Her exposure to these healthier families gave her hope that she too could perhaps have a loving family much different from the one she grew up with as a young child.

Once in professional recovery, what are tools that helped Pam stay focused? The first two tools that come to her mind that helped her in staying focused were keeping a recovery notebook and keeping a journal.

What is a recovery notebook? A recovery notebook tracks events and progress through recovery. It can contain anything the person in recovery wants. Pam's included informational handouts given to her by her therapists, completed homework assignments from her therapist, such as letters written to former perpetrators and other memorabilia from her recovery journey. In her case, Pam's therapist asked her to share the contents with her, which she willingly did do to help her therapist track her progress.

What about a recovery journal is different from a recovery notebook? One difference in Pam's case was that sharing her recovery journal with her therapist was optional. Journals and diaries are intended for one's personal use, more confidential in nature. They help persons in recovery vent feelings, sort through memories,

> **"A recovery notebook tracks events and progress through recovery. It can contain anything the person in recovery wants."**

and track one's progress. At least, that's what they did for Pam in her recovery. Later, she used her journal entries in writing the memoirs, *Freedom in Truth*. She also includes a few journal entries in this book.

What else motivated Pam to stay focused in her recovery? Other factors that motivated Pam to move forward in recovery were seeing better ways of living exemplified in the lives of others in her environment and also reading the testimonials included in the many self-help books that she read along her journey. Both of these things gave her insight into healthier ways of living and a hope that her life could be better if she did the work needed to recover, not only from being a victim of generational sins but also from the consequences of her own sins and mistakes in reaction to her traumatic past.

Goal setting is helpful in staying focused on moving forward in recovery.

> *There is great value in setting goals in recovery. The goal-setting process builds confidence, boosts self-esteem, promotes discipline, and encourages healthy living. Being intentional about life and achieving goals deepens our sense of purpose.* [2]

Orgeron recommends clients in recovery use **SMART** goals in their recovery process. What are SMART goals? "SMART" in recovery is an acronym for "**S**elf-**M**anagement **a**nd **R**ecovery **T**raining". Additionally,

> *In SMART Goal Setting, SMART embodies five key characteristics of effective goals: Specific, Measurable, Agreeable, Realistic, and Time-bound. These attributes ensure your goals are clear, attainable, and aligned with your recovery path.*

1. *Specific*
   Specificity in goal setting involves clearly defining what you aim to achieve. Broad goals like "I want to feel happier" are a start, but they lack the detail necessary to guide actionable steps. A more specific goal might be, "I will engage in a hobby I enjoy for at least an hour three times a week."

2. *Measurable*
   A goal is measurable when you can objectively assess whether it's been met. This often involves quantifiable metrics, like frequency, amounts, or durations. For example, "I will attend two support meetings per week" is a measurable goal.

3. *Agreeable*
   Your goals should be agreeable, meaning they resonate with your inner values, desires, and personal recovery commitments. They should be goals you are willing and intending to pursue, ensuring they're aligned with your personal vision for your life and recovery.

4. *Realistic*
   Realistic goals are those within the realm of possibility. They stretch you beyond your comfort zone but still remain achievable based on your current resources, circumstances, and commitments. An unrealistic goal sets you up for failure, while a realistic goal fosters motivation and progress.

> 5. Time-bound
> Goals need a deadline or time frame. Whether it's a daily goal like "I will practice mindfulness after breakfast every day" or a long-term goal like "I will complete a recovery workbook within three months," time constraints create urgency and promote accountability.[3]

In addition to utilizing the principles advocated by SMART Recovery, Orgeron further recommends that those in recovery replace long-term goals with short-term goals. In other words, break down long-term goals into smaller increments that once reached can be rewarded to motivate one to continue progress. To exemplify this process in Orgeron's life she thinks of how she lost 80 pounds over about a year and a half. Instead, of saying up front, "I'm going to lose 80 pounds," what she did was to break that long-term goal down into losing 5 to 10 pounds at a time in a shorter period of time. Rewards might have included purchasing a new self-help book or buying a new outfit after her clothes became too big. Doing that helped motivate her to stay focused on continuing to eat healthily and to exercise regularly as she was doing to lose weight.

> "...replace long-term goals with short-term goals. In other words, break down long-term goals into smaller increments that once reached can be rewarded to motivate one to continue progress."

To summarize this chapter, Orgeron reminds those working to overcome generational curses that the journey will not be easy. Storms and obstacles will come and go throughout the process but by staying focused and keeping one's eyes on the "prize", one can overcome.

" ¹³ Brethren, I do not count myself to have apprehended; but one thing I do, forgetting those things which are behind and reaching forward to those things which are ahead, ¹⁴ I press toward the goal for the prize of the upward call of God in Christ Jesus" (Philippians 3:13-14).

***

Notes

[1] WestBridge, How to Stay Focused on Your Goals in Recovery, ¶ 1, Retrieved January 14, 2024 from https://www.westbridge.org/how-to-stay-focused-on-your-goals-in-recovery/

[2] Ashley Addiction Treatment, Setting SMART Goals in Recovery, The Reality of Resolutions-Most People Don't Cross the Finish Line section, ¶ 3, Retrieved January 15, 2024 from https://www.ashleytreatment.org/rehab-blog/setting-smart-goals-in-recovery/#:

[3] SMART Recovery, Setting SMART Goals, Decoding SMART Goals section, Retrieved January 15, 2024 from https://smartrecovery.org/setting-smart-goals#:

Pamela K. Orgeron, M.A., Ed.S., BCCC, ACLC, BCMMHC

CHAPTER 18

Be Aware of Your Weaknesses

Knowing one's weaknesses, which Orgeron also equates to barriers and triggers, is a key to being able to move forward in overcoming the effects of generational or personal sins.

> *Barriers to recovery can consist of internal factors, such as character defects and negative emotional states, and external factors such as high-risk situations and events. Whether internal or external, these barriers can trigger relapse. Once you understand your personal triggers, you can plan how you will respond to them—and thereby protect your recovery.* [1]

One of the first keys Pam learned from her first therapist to prevent her from progressing in recovery was the acronym **HALT**. Her therapist encouraged her not to get too *h*ungry, too *a*ngry, too *l*onely, or too *t*ired. Any of these conditions, could lead to relapse, her therapist said.

Being around "toxic" people also can serve as a big stumbling block in recovery. Who are toxic people? They are people in one's life who may either intentionally or unintentionally hinder or discourage recovery. Keeping a distance and setting strong healthy boundaries are important in dealing with such relationships. Orgeron remembers for quite a while after she first entered therapy her therapist advised her to have no contact with her biological family of origin, particularly her mother who had been previously diagnosed with a mental illness. This period of abstinence from her family gave Pam time to heal and time to learn new coping skills in dealing with dysfunctional attitudes and behaviors of her family.

For some victims in recovery letting go of toxic relationships can be hard. What do these people need to remember?

> *One of the most difficult parts of this journey is to let go of old relationships. But, toxins from substance abuse are not the only harmful part of addiction—just like drugs or alcohol were bad for your physical health, toxic people are bad for your mental wellbeing. Especially your old "friends" who were a negative influence and could become a hindrance as you're trying to start fresh.*
>
> *Removing toxic people from your life is often much more difficult than removing toxins from your body. Don't feel bad about breaking up these relationships.* [2]

In Christian contexts, Orgeron would refer to weaknesses that could hinder recovery as temptations. What does the Scripture say about temptation? Temptation, in and of itself, is not bad or sinful. How one reacts to temptation determines whether one has sinned. What are the sources of temptation? There are three identified in the Scriptures: the flesh (James 1:13-15), the world (Galatians 1:4, 2 Peter 1:4, 1 John 2:15) and Satan (Ephesians 6:12). Orgeron believes Satan is the ultimate tempter and enemy faced by those in recovery. Christ Himself referred to Satan as the enemy in Luke 10:19.

How should victims in recovery from generational and personal sins deal with triggers and temptations? Though some people advise others to avoid any type of trigger or temptation, this advice is not realistic. Nobody can control everything in their path or environment so to think anyone can eliminate all triggers and temptations from their life is unrealistic. Orgeron believes that the key to dealing with triggers and temptations lies in facing the issues and having a predetermined plan as to how to deal with triggers and temptations when they arise. Since Orgeron never dealt with the vices of promiscuity, alcohol, illegal drugs, or tobacco personally, she uses the aforementioned key to help her avoid overeating like she used to do. How so?

First, Orgeron knows that eating out, especially at buffets, tempts her to overeat. Since eating at a buffet is not considered a necessity in life, she chooses not to eat out where the restaurant has a buffet. That choice is based on Scriptures that instructs Christians to flee evil and temptation (Proverbs 4:14-15; 2 Timothy 2:22).

Another setting in particular that Pam found particularly tempting and a risk to her relapsing into overeating during recovery was at holiday meals, especially Thanksgiving and Christmas. As a child growing up, her family's norm was to always go back for seconds at a holiday meal and always have sugary desserts. That was an easy habit for her to learn, and difficult to break as she recovered.

> **"Temptation, in and of itself, is not bad or sinful. How one reacts to temptation determines whether one has sinned."**

Over the years of recovering Pam struggled with a lot of issues to overcome being overweight and overeating. She wrestled with many questions: Is it worth eating when she was not hungry just to avoid offending someone pushing her to eat? Her conclusion: NO, it was not selfish to consider her needs and take care of herself.

Inactivity also contributed to Pam being overweight in her younger years. Her mother always spoke of how she hated exercise and passed this prejudice on to her daughter. Pam had to adopt new attitudes towards exercising. Her first therapist told her that the key was to find an exercise that she enjoys doing. Pam always enjoyed riding bikes as a child. Now she regularly works out daily on a stationary bike.

Due to her new attitudes and behaviors surrounding diet and exercise (exercise suppresses the appetite), this past Christmas Orgeron had no struggles with feeling tempted to overeat. What made the difference? She had a pre-determined plan that she developed years ago regarding how to deal with holiday meals; she would only allow herself to eat no more than what she could fit on one plate the first time around. Additionally, she and her husband have chosen to cook healthier entrees than what her family of origin cooked. For example, instead of fixing sweet potato casserole with all the nuts and sugar like her mother made, they have baked sweet potatoes for their Thanksgiving and Christmas dinners for the past several years. This past Christmas Orgeron even chose to forego having any dessert with their meal. Talk about discipline!

For most sins of addiction, total abstinence is what Orgeron recommends. Examples of such addictions include alcohol, drugs, smoking, gambling, etc. However, as most people know, one must eat to live. Thus, total abstinence is not the answer to overcoming any type of food addiction. Self-control and having a predetermined plan of what to do in tempting situations are keys to a successful recovery. For example, Pam made the decision years ago not to eat sugary desserts, regardless of who offers them to her. So now when offered desserts made with real sugar, she politely refuses the offer, saying, "No, thank you. I don't eat sweets".

13 No temptation has overtaken you except such as is common to man; but God is faithful, who will not allow you

Pamela K. Orgeron, M.A., Ed.S., BCCC, ACLC, BCMMHC

to be tempted beyond what you are able, but with the temptation will also make the way of escape, that you may be able to bear it (1 Corinthians 10:13-15).

***

Notes

¹ Oregon Recovery & Treatment Centers, ¶ 1, Retrieved January 15, 2024 from https://ortc.care/blog/barriers-to-recovery/#:

² Olalia Recovery Centers, Avoiding Toxic People During Recovery, ¶s 2-3. Retrieved January 15, 2024 from https://www.olalla.org/addiction-recovery-blog/avoiding-toxic-people-during-recovery/

CHAPTER 19

Utilize and Focus on Your Strengths

A strength-based approach to recovery from generational curses focuses on the assets rather than the liabilities of the person in recovery. These assets could include factors such as certain personality traits (e.g., honesty), interests, natural talents, and resources.

> *When you know your strengths, you can call on them during challenging moments in life. A better understanding of what makes you strong opens your possibilities, placing you in circumstances that can accelerate your personal or professional life. Your strengths help you maintain a healthy, positive life.* [1]

Orgeron also believes what some would consider negative traits or liabilities can be utilized as strengths. For example, consider obsessive compulsive traits. Being obsessive compulsive generally is considered unhealthy. However, Orgeron believes without her obsessive compulsive disorder passed down from her mother she would not have been as successful academically and professionally.

What are the advantages of knowing one's strengths? Renaissance Ranch Treatment Centers reported the following benefits to recognizing one's strengths:

Pamela K. Orgeron, M.A., Ed.S., BCCC, ACLC, BCMMHC

- *Your focus is on those things that will positively impact your life. For example, if you know your strength lies in being compassionate, you can volunteer or work for an organization that helps those in need. Working with or helping others can boost your mental health.*
- *You can use your time efficiently when you know what you excel at.*
- *Your strengths can aid you in valuing yourself, raising your standards, and expecting more in life.*
- *Acknowledging and focusing on your strengths means you can make smarter decisions about your relationships, goals, and environment. Another upside to knowing where you excel is choosing a career that will thrive because of your knowledge, skills, and abilities.*
- *The goals you create will also benefit from focusing on your natural abilities. Then, as you plan to achieve your goal, you can design a straightforward course of action that uses your talents, saves you time, and decreases stress if obstacles come between you and your purpose.*[2]

What were the strengths that Pam benefited from that prevented her from ending up in an early grave like other persons experiencing similar abuse at an early age? She believes that she possessed cognitive and personality traits, interests, natural talents, and resources that aided her in overcoming the generational curses in her life.

Intelligence, a cognitive trait, was recognized by Pam's father in her at a young age. Thus, he pushed her academically to fulfill his and later her dream of going to college. No one else in her family had ever attended college. She was a first-generation college graduate. Throughout her school years math and science came easy to her prompting her to take more of those courses in high school. She graduated co-salutatorian.

When the time came to choose a career, Pam's lifelong interests in reading and writing overshadowed her doing well in math and science. Remember how she had told her grandmother at a young age that she wanted to be a writer because that way she could tell more people about Jesus. Remember the diary she kept that was destroyed by her mother.

Listening to the peer pressure of others, Pam started college as a Banking Management major, and then switched to Mathematics, with an emphasis in teaching. That did not last long. She ended up graduating with an undergraduate degree in journalism-public relations, with minors in English, psychology, and political science. Later, she completed a master's and Education Specialist Degree in Adult & Higher Education, Counseling Specialization.

The character traits of honesty and being caring and compassionate made counseling a good fit for Pam. These traits combined with her educational background and personal experiences of having overcome past abuse and trauma have enabled her to encourage and teach others what she has learned through her struggles. Her desire is to apply her educational background with her personal experience to minister to others recovering from past abuse and trauma.

Pam also has natural talents that she has found doing are very therapeutic for her. Besides writing, other talents she possesses are sewing, making crafts, quilting, and cooking. She took home economics that gave her the foundation for most of these skills that come natural to her. Her parents bought her a sewing machine for Christmas the year she took home economics. She still owns and uses that machine whenever she takes a notion to sew now. Additionally, she had the role models of her paternal grandmother and one of her maternal aunts who additionally taught her sewing and quilting techniques. As cooking role models, most of the women in both sides of her family were great cooks. She learned as much as she could from each of them.

What other resources did Pam have to help her in moving along towards reaching her goals? She took advantage of available educational grants to complete her undergraduate degree. In graduate school, she survived financially through part-time work, student loans, and assistance from a few friends.

Two additional character traits of Pam that worked to her advantage in recovery are being frugal and being responsible. She has never been one to waste money, or anything for that matter. She and her husband eat leftovers from meals. Often, especially for holiday meals, they make frozen TV dinners that they put in the freezer to prevent food spoilage and to eat another time. In addition to trying to avoid the temptation of Pam overeating, they rarely eat out at restaurants because they find it more economical to cook and eat at home.

Being responsible is a key that helped Pam succeed academically and towards recovery. She does not remember a time that she did not complete a homework assignment given by a teacher, or even a therapist later when in psychotherapy. In fact, she always made an effort to complete assignments as soon as possible. She would even turn assignments in early if the teacher permitted her to do so. She remembers in writing her senior high school research paper, she was the first student to complete the assignment. Her senior English teacher accepted her paper before the due date. Those are examples of how she took advantage of the obsessive compulsiveness in her nature.

Overcoming Generational Curses

What does Orgeron consider her greatest asset in overcoming past generational curses and personal failures? Nothing but the presence of the Holy Spirit in her life through the gift of Salvation! She has no doubt about that! She believes that being able to live with and ultimately overcome generational curses is only possible through Christ. Why? Because being abused makes one vulnerable to demonic influences! She knows that from personal experience. She recalls two times when she has no doubt, demons were physically attacking her. The first attack happened one night when she was startled awake by an evil presence on top of her trying to choke her. In a few moments she realized what was happening. She started praying aloud and rebuking Satan in the name of Jesus Christ. Immediately the evil presence left.

> "...being able to live with and ultimately overcome generational curses is only possible through Christ. Why? Because being abused makes one vulnerable to demonic influences!"

The second demonic attack was one evening when she was getting ready to attend a church function. She started feeling sick, like she was going to throw up. She knew there was absolutely no physical reason why she should be sick at her stomach, as she was taking medication for GERD. When she got into the bathroom, she developed an intense headache. The thought crossed her mind, *this is a satanic attack.* Immediately, she rebuked Satan in the name of Jesus. Guess what happened? Immediately the headache was gone and she was no longer sick.

In closing this chapter, Orgeron encourages Christians to use their best asset of being able to pray as their primary weapon and defense to overcome the consequences of generational curses and the effects of personal sin in one's life.

Pamela K. Orgeron, M.A., Ed.S., BCCC, ACLC, BCMMHC

> "⁵Trust in the LORD with all your heart,
> And lean not on your own understanding;
> ⁶ In all your ways acknowledge Him,
> And He shall direct your paths"
> (Proverbs 3:5-6).

***

Notes

[1] Renaissance Ranch Treatment Centers, Assessing Strengths and Weaknesses in Recovery, ¶ 2, Retrieved January 16, 2024 from https://renaissanceranch.net/assessing-strengths-and-weaknesses-in-recovery/#:

[2] Renaissance Ranch Treatment Centers, Assessing Strengths and Weaknesses in Recovery, The Benefits of Having Clarity in Your Strengths section, Retrieved January 16, 2024 from https://renaissanceranch.net/assessing-strengths-and-weaknesses-in-recovery/#

CHAPTER 20

Be an Advocate for Others

" ³ Blessed be the God and Father of our Lord Jesus Christ, the Father of mercies and God of all comfort, ⁴ who comforts us in all our tribulation, that we may be able to comfort those who are in any trouble, with the comfort with which we ourselves are comforted by God" (2 Corinthians 1:3-4, NKJV).

The above Scripture is the key verse that freed Orgeron to share her story of having been abused, her unhealthy, sinful reactions to the abuse (e.g.: overeating), and the details of her recovery journey. She used to be very uncomfortable sharing her weaknesses with others until she became aware of 2 Corinthians 1:3-4 and of the dysfunctional beliefs shared in a previous chapter that she had been taught as a child. Now she has few reservations sharing her testimony, her story of recovery as a part of her ministry.

What victims and survivors need to understand is that God may have allowed the specific generational curses they live with to prepare them for a special ministry, based on 2 Corinthians 1:3-4. Two instances in Pam's life taught her that.

"Setbacks are often setups for special ministries." Orgeron said she will never forget hearing that statement from a radio minister years ago when she was facing trials.

Secondly, Oregon says that she also will never forget the wise advice given to her by former Singles Minister of Two Rivers Baptist Church, Seton Tomyn, when she asked him why God had allowed her crushed left ankle and its aftermath. He directed her to read 2 Corinthians, Chapter 1. Since reading and realizing the truths of that Scripture and seeing how the truth lived out in her own life later, it's not hard for her to find peace in any situation she faces.

> "What victims and survivors need to understand is that God may have allowed the specific generational curses they live with to prepare them for a special ministry, based on 2 Corinthians 1:3-4."

One of the first places that Orgeron recommends where survivors can share their testimony to advocate and encourage others is in a 12-step recovery group, preferably Christian based. She has shared her testimony of recovery a number of times at different Celebrate Recovery (CR) groups. In addition to CR groups, Orgeron also recommends those needing help to look at the Life Recovery website, to find any such group in their area, if available.

The last step of any 12-step support group typically involves reaching out to others. For example,

> 12. Having had a spiritual awakening as a result of these steps, we tried to carry this message to others, and to practice these principles in all our affairs.
>
> "Dear brothers and sisters, if another believer is overcome by some sin, you who are godly should gently and humbly help that person back onto the right path. And be careful not to fall into the same

temptation yourself." – Galatians 6:1; see also Isaiah 61:1-3; Titus 3:3-7; 1 Peter 4:1-5.[1]

Another Scripture reference that Orgeron believes should encourage survivors to reach out to help others is "Bear one another's burdens, and so fulfill the law of Christ" (Galatians 6:2, NKJV). What are ways survivors can serve or help others bear burdens? Remember too that in the aftermath of recovering from any trauma, God can use an individual not only in ministering to those with similar experiences but to others in a myriad of ways. Orgeron offers a few suggestions: volunteer at a local homeless shelter, hospital, or nursing home; give financially to a favorite charity; volunteer at church (e.g.: teach a Sunday school class), or even help an elderly or disabled neighbor with chores or running errands.

In addition to volunteering in practical ways mentioned previously, victims can become involved in political activist groups related to one's area of pain. For example, an individual who has had a child killed by a drunk driver might want to get involved in the Mothers against Drunk Drivers organization. Some victims may choose careers related to what happened to them. An example of this would be an abused child who grows up to work as a social worker or counselor with abused children.

Remember helping others also helps further oneself along in life and recovery. How so? Here are some benefits to serving:
- Volunteering produces dopamine in the brain, which elevates one's mood.
- Helping others creates a sense of community with others.
- Volunteering gives one a sense of purpose, a reason for living.
- Volunteering, especially with the homeless, can lead to an attitude of gratitude.

- Helping others often creates a ripple effect, and as one of Pam's aunts told her years ago, "Kindness always comes back to you".
- Volunteering may help reduce stress, which can increase one's longevity.
- Volunteering could open doors into something permanent that produces income,
- Volunteering could alleviate loneliness by creating opportunities to create new friendships and develop old relationships.

> *Being of service to others and participating with others in a group to better the world can lift our spirits. It can also have real-world effects on our bodies. As you keep your brain and body active, you ward off cognitive decline and keep yourself healthy.*[2]

Before closing this chapter, Orgeron would feel amiss not to share the following two Scriptures:

"[23] And whatever you do, do it heartily, as to the Lord and not to men, [24] knowing that from the Lord you will receive the reward of the inheritance; for you serve the Lord Christ" (Colossians 3:23-24, NKJV).

"[10] For God is not unjust to forget your work and labor of love which you have shown toward His name, in that you have ministered to the saints, and do minister" (Hebrews 6:10, NKJV).

"Remember helping others also helps further oneself along in life and recovery."

To close this chapter, Orgeron would like to encourage other survivors of generational curses to consider whether God is calling them to a special ministry of service. If so, she encourages them to be obedient to that call, remembering,

"²⁴He who calls you is faithful, who also will do it"
(1 Thessalonians 5:24, NKJV).

***

Notes

[1] Life Recovery Groups, The 12 Steps, Step 12, Retrieved January 16, 2024 from https://liferecoverygroups.com/the-12-steps/

[2] Field, What Are the Mental Health Benefits of Volunteering? Physical Health Benefits of Volunteering section, ¶ 2, Retrieved January 16, 2024 from https://www.verywellmind.com/what-are-the-mental-health-benefits-of-volunteering-5248549#toc-mental-health-benefits-of-volunteering

CHAPTER 21

Above All, Sow in the Spirit, NOT the Flesh

"[7] Do not be deceived, God is not mocked; for whatever a man sows, that he will also reap. [8] For he who sows to his flesh will of the flesh reap corruption, but he who sows to the Spirit will of the Spirit reap everlasting life. [9] And let us not grow weary while doing good, for in due season we shall reap if we do not lose heart. [10] Therefore, as we have opportunity, let us do good to all, especially to those who are of the household of faith" (Galatians 6:7-10).

What does the phrase "sow in the spirit" mean? Orgeron describes this phenomenon as living a lifestyle directed by the Holy Spirit manifesting the fruit of the Spirit. What is the fruit of the Spirit?

"[22] But the fruit of the Spirit is love, joy, peace, longsuffering, kindness, goodness, faithfulness, [23] gentleness, self-control. Against such there is no law" (Galatians 5:22-23).

How does Scripture describe sowing in the flesh?

"[19] Now the works of the flesh are evident, which are: adultery, fornication, uncleanness, lewdness, [20] idolatry, sorcery, hatred, contentions,

> *jealousies, outbursts of wrath, selfish ambitions, dissensions, heresies, [21] envy, murders, drunkenness, revelries, and the like; of which I tell you beforehand, just as I also told you in time past, that those who practice such things will not inherit the kingdom of God"*
> *(Galatians 5:19-21).*

Though the Holy Spirit is a Christian's ultimate guide to living in God's will, what can one do to increase the odds that he or she will not submit to fleshly desires and behaviors? Orgeron believes there are a number of actions people can do to prepare for and resist temptation. Most of these actions fall under at least one of two domains: practicing the spiritual disciplines, and putting on the armor of God.

The Spiritual Disciplines. All Christians are called to live a holy life (1 Peter 1:16). Spiritual disciplines are tools to help Christians live out a life of holiness. Donald S. Whitney, a professor at The Southern Baptist Theological Seminary, Louisville, KY and author of *Spiritual Disciplines for the Christian Life* (NavPress, 1991, 2014), defines them as,

> *"those practices found in Scripture that promote spiritual growth among believers in the gospel of Jesus Christ. They are habits of devotion, habits of experiential Christianity that have been practiced by God's people since biblical times."* [1]

Given the definition, Whitney identifies the characteristics of a spiritual discipline. These characteristics include:
- The Scriptures advocate both individual and corporate practices (e.g. personal prayer and corporate prayer)
- Spiritual disciplines are activities, things one does.
- All spiritual disciplines were taught or exemplified in Scripture. To further clarify, activities, such as gardening or

exercise, are NOT spiritual disciplines, as some might consider.
- Spiritual disciplines are adequate in developing a life of holiness, or godliness. They are

> *"derived from the gospel, not divorced from the gospel. Rightly practiced, the spiritual disciplines take us deeper into the glories of the gospel of Jesus Christ, not away from it as though we have moved on to some advanced level of Christianity,"* [2]

- Christians are told to exercise, or discipline themselves toward godliness (1 Timothy 4:7). This implies that the spiritual disciplines are the way, or path to becoming holy, or godly, not the end result. So, according to Whitney,

> *"we are not godly just because we practice the spiritual disciplines. That was the great error of the Pharisees. They felt by doing these things they were godly. No, they are means to godliness. Rightly motivated, they are the means to godliness."* [3]

How many spiritual disciplines are there? The number varies, depending on the author. Based on the characteristics given by Whitney, among the spiritual disciplines most helpful to Orgeron are:
- Prayer (Individual, 1 Thessalonians 5:17; Corporate, Genesis 4:26)
- Fasting (Individual, Luke 18:12; Corporate, Ezra 8:23)
- Bible Study (Individual, 2 Timothy 2:15; Corporate, Acts 17:11)

Putting on the Armor of God. Paul told the Ephesians,

"¹⁰ Finally, my brethren, be strong in the Lord and in the power of His might. ¹¹ Put on the whole armor of God, that you may be able to stand against the wiles of the devil" (Ephesians 6:10-11).

What makes up the "full armor of God"? Ephesians 6:14-18 describes God's armor:

"¹⁴ Stand therefore, having girded your waist with truth, having put on the breastplate of righteousness, ¹⁵ and having shod your feet with the preparation of the gospel of peace; ¹⁶ above all, taking the shield of faith with which you will be able to quench all the fiery darts of the wicked one. ¹⁷ And take the helmet of salvation, and the sword of the Spirit, which is the word of God; ¹⁸ praying always with all prayer and supplication in the Spirit, being watchful to this end with all perseverance and supplication for all the saints (NKJV).

Orgeron believes that individuals suffering the effects of generational curses will find deeper healing through incorporating spiritual disciplines in their lives and by putting on the full armor of God. Only by doing so can they overcome the attacks and temptations of Satan that would hinder recovery.

How should those in recovery react to family members and others who refuse to accept the truth continuing to live in sinful or at least unhealthy ways? Pam shares her past experiences to answer this question?

"There's a difference between loving a person and not liking a person's behavior," Psychologist Kathryn Sherrod, Ph.D. said to Pam years ago. "You can love a person without liking a person's behavior, and that's okay."

Prior to hearing and making sense of Dr. Sherrod's comment above, Pam struggled with a lot of false guilt for not liking unbiblical attitudes and/or behavior patterns of others whom she also loved.

> **"There's a difference between loving a person and not liking a person's behavior. You can love a person without liking a person's behavior, and that is okay."—Kathy Sherrod, Psychologist**

No doubt parents also should be able to identify with the concept of loving the sinner and hating the sin. When a child disobeys, Orgeron believes that the child him or herself should not be criticized but the emphasis needs to be put on the behavior that is bad. Statements such as, "You're being bad," "Shame on you," and "You're mean" are detrimental to a child's self-esteem and heard often enough can result in what psychologists call *self-fulfilled prophecy*. With a self-fulfilled prophecy, when a person hears a statement enough times, he or she begins to believe the statement and the false statement becomes a part of the person's identity. Rather than attacking the person of a misbehaving child, the specific offense should be emphasized as being wrong and what the parent does not like.

To both exemplify the concept of "love the sinner, hate the sin" and to voice a word of caution against enabling unhealthy behaviors, Orgeron shares the following account not intended as a put down to those who are homeless or meant to imply that the homeless are not as good as those blessed to have homes and other luxuries. There is no sin in being homeless. Pam has been in the position of being homeless more than once. Jesus Christ Himself also was homeless.

Orgeron remembers a former Sunday school teacher sharing in one of his classes, "Never give money to a homeless person. In doing so, you may be putting yourself in a position where you are condoning sinful behaviors." He also shared how a homeless person had approached him asking for money. What he did rather than giving the person money, he asked the person what he wanted the money for. When the gentlemen told Pam's Sunday school teacher that he was hungry and had not eaten for days, her Sunday school teacher took the homeless man in a nearby restaurant, bought him a meal, and more than likely shared the Gospel with him. What a mature attitude and example of being Christ like in living.

Often Orgeron sees homeless individuals out smoking and carrying a bottle of alcohol while asking for money. Since hearing the advice of her former Sunday school teacher, she quit giving money to such individuals. In an effort to show the love of Christ to the homeless, what she has done is give them food and/or pray for them. Many years ago as a single woman, she opened her home for two homeless women at different times that were referred to her by a church to try to help. Later, her husband and she let a homeless man sleep on their couch and gave him the opportunity to take a shower and wash his clothes. In recent years, she and her husband opened their home to both a male and a female who were in recovery simultaneously. Of course, Pam and her husband do not allow any individuals staying in their home to smoke or have alcohol in their home. Nor do they allow profanity. They also do not allow unmarried persons of the opposite sex to share sleeping quarters. To do so, they would have been going against deep-seated religious convictions and disobeying God's Word (Ephesians 5:1-7).

Hating sin, even the sins of one's forefathers, and the consequences created by such sin is not wrong (Psalm 97:10; Proverbs 8:13; Amos 5:15). Also, remember these generational curses can be overcome. One way to help those in recovery is to reach out and help others without condoning, ignoring, making excuses for, or enabling the sins of others. Christians enable sin by encouraging, empowering, or making it easier for one to participate in sin. This contradicts the Christian's call to righteousness and holiness.

"[40] And the King will answer and say to them, 'Assuredly, I say to you, inasmuch as you did it to one of the least of these My brethren, you did it to Me'" (Matthew 25:40).

***

Notes

[1] Whitney, D. S. (Speaker). (2015). What are spiritual disciplines? (Interview Episode 762). ¶ 4, Minneapolis, MN: Desiring God Foundation. Retrieved January 17, 2024 from https://www.desiringgod.org/interviews/what-are-spiritual-disciplines

[2] Whitney, D. S. (Speaker). (2015). What are spiritual disciplines? Section 5. Derived from the Gospel, ¶ 1 (Interview Episode 762). Minneapolis, MN: Desiring God Foundation. Retrieved January 17, 2024 from https://www.desiringgod.org/interviews/what-are-spiritual-disciplines

[3] Whitney, D. S. (Speaker). (2015). What are spiritual disciplines? Section 6. Means, Not End, ¶ 2, (Interview Episode 762). Minneapolis, MN: Desiring God Foundation. Retrieved January 17, 2024 from https://www.desiringgod.org/interviews/what-are-spiritual-disciplines

CHAPTER 22

Final Reflections: "Good Triumphs Evil"

"What have you learned from all this?" a professional therapist in the counseling field asked the author about six years ago after she shared her experience of witnessing her grandfather's atrocious acts.

"I don't know," Orgeron replied.

"Yes, you do," she said. "You've learned that good triumphs evil. Look at all you have accomplished and how God is blessing you."

"Thinking about it that way," Orgeron said. "You're right."

God has allowed good to triumph evil in Orgeron's life in so many ways. He has brought about miracles in answering prayers, in particular allowing her and her parents to be at peace with each other whenever they both passed. Of special significance to Orgeron, her mother had undergone shock treatments to make her forget her part of the murder cover up. However, she finally remembered about the murder and the conspiracy that followed before her passing to apologize for the way her daughter had been hurt by what happened. However, many in the family remain in denial about what happened. That is their choice to make; but, Orgeron will continue to stand for the truth and use what she has learned to minister to others. She can only pray for those who remain in denial.

While many who have experienced traumas similar to what the author went through as a young child ended up as prostitutes, on drugs, in jail, and even worse, she was blessed to do well academically, to fulfill her dream of becoming a writer, and of creating a home full of love and peace alongside her wonderful husband. What made the difference? No doubt, nothing other than the presence of God in her life made the difference.

Throughout *Overcoming Generational Curses* Pam Orgeron (aka, Pam Owens) has shared much of her life story, her heart. She has shared the major hurts in her childhood and the tools provided by God to overcome the consequences of those injuries. She encourages others negatively affected by generational sin to apply the tools suggested in this book, realizing that each person's story is unique and what works for one person might not help another.

The author hopes other victims will find encouragement from this book to turn their hearts to Jesus who can bring triumph over any tragedy. Just as He allowed good to triumph evil in the author's life, He is able to do the same for anyone who submits to Him. Orgeron hopes and prays that God blesses each one reading this book with a victorious Christian life and witness.

***

RECOMMENDED RESOURCES

The following listed resources are what helped the author as she walked the road to recovery from being an insecure victim to being a confident victor in Jesus Christ. She also includes more recent resources that she has become familiar with since her recovery and that other professionals have brought to her attention.

Articles/Books

Codependency

Beattie, M. (1989). *Beyond codependency and getting better all the time.* San Francisco: Harper & Row.
Beattie, M. (1987). *Codependent no more.* USA: Hazelden.
Jantz, G. L., & Clinton, T. (2015). *Don't call it love: Breaking the cycle of relationship dependency.* Grand Rapids, MI: Revell.
Springle, P. (1990). *Close enough to care, helping a friend or relative overcome codependency.* Houston & Dallas, Texas: Rapha & Word.

Complex PTSD

Beauty After Bruises (n.d.). *Beauty after bruises...bringing light back into the eyes of survivors with Complex PTSD and Dissociative Trauma Disorders* [Website Home Page]. Retrieved January 21, 2024 from https://www.beautyafterbruises.org/home
Beauty After Bruises (n.d.). *What is C-PTSD?.* Retrieved January 21, 2024 from https://www.beautyafterbruises.org/what-is-cptsd/
BetterHelp (2023). *What is Complex PTSD?* Retrieved January 21, 2024 from https://www.betterhelp.com/advice/ptsd/what-is-complex-ptsd/

The Center for Treatment of Anxiety & Mood Disorders (2022). *Complex PTSD*. Retrieved January 21, 2024 from http://centerforanxietydisorders.com/complex-ptsd/

Herman, J. L. (1992). Complex PTSD: A syndrome in survivors of prolonged and repeated trauma. *Journal of Traumatic Stress, 5*(3), 377–391.

Herman, J. L. (1997). *Trauma and recovery: The aftermath of violence—From domestic to political terror*. New York: Basic Books.

Lucario, L. H. (n.d.). *Healing from complex trauma & PTSD/CPTSD: A journey to healing from complex trauma* [Website Home Page]. Retrieved January 21, 2024 from https://healingfromcomplextraumaandptsd.wordpress.com/

Lucario, L. H. (2023). *12 life-impacting symptoms complex PTSD survivors endure*. Retrieved January 21, 2024 from https://themighty.com/2017/08/life-impacting-symptoms-of-complex-post-traumatic-stress-disorder-ptsd/

Nicholas, E. (2015). *The living nightmare of complex post-traumatic disorder*. Retrieved January 21, 2024 from https://www.vice.com/en_us/article/vdxjn8/worse-than-ptsd-the-nightmare-of-complex-post-traumatic-stress-disorder

Walker, P. (2014). *Complex PTSD: From Surviving to Thriving*. USA: Peter Walker.

Wright, H. N. (2003). *The new guide to crisis and trauma counseling*. Ventura, CA: Regal.

Wright, H. N. (2008). *Surviving the storms of life: Finding hope and healing when life goes wrong*. Grand Rapids, MI: Revell.

Disordered Eating

Andersen, A., Cohn, L., & Holbrook, T. (2000). *Making weight: Men's conflicts with food, weight, shape & appearance*. Carlsbad, CA: Gurze.

Anonymous (1989). *Take it off and keep it off: Based on the successful methods of overeaters anonymous.*Chicago: Contemporary.

Arterburn, S., & Lamphear, V. (1979, 1980, 1982). *Gentle eating workbook*. Nashville: Nelson.

Baker, C. (1995). *Fed up: college students & eating problems*. New York: Bold.

Gaesser, G. A. (2002). *Big fat lies: The truth about your weight and your health* (Updated ed.). Carlsbad, CA: Gurze.

Gaesser, G. A., & Kratina, K. (2000). *Eating well, living well when you can't diet anymore: A guide to help you reach your personal health goal.* Parker, CO: Wheat Foods Council.

Glennon, W. (2000). *200 ways to raise a boy's emotional intelligence: An indispensable guide for parents, teachers, and other concerned caregivers.* Berkeley: Conari.

Greene, B. (2002), *Get with the program: Getting real about your health, weight, and emotional well-being.* New York: Simon & Schuster.

Hirschmann, J. R., & Munter, C. H. (1988). *Overcoming Overeating.* New York: Ballantine.

Hirschmann, J. R., & Zaphiropoulos, L. (1993). *Preventing childhood eating problems: A practical, positive approach to raising children free of food & weight conflicts.* Carlsbad, CA: Gurze.

Homme, M. (1999). *Seeing yourself in God's image: Overcoming anorexia and bulimia.* Chattanooga: Turning Point.

McGraw, P. C. (2003). *The ultimate weight solution: The 7 keys to weight loss freedom.* New York: Free Press.

Minirth, F. B.., Meier, P. D., Hemfelt, R., Sneed, S., & Hawkins, D. (1990). *Love hunger: Recovery from food addiction.* Nashville: Thomas Nelson.

Orgeron, P. K. (2017). *Food as an idol: Finding freedom from disordered eating.* Nashville, TN: ABC's Ministries.

Orgeron, P. K. (2019). *Food as an idol: The types, causes, consequences, conquering, and prevention of disordered eating.* Nashville, TN: ABC's Ministries.

Pritikin Staff (2024). Unhealthy Weight Loss or Gain from Eating Disorders. Retrieved January 22, 2024 from https://www.pritikin.com/articles/unhealthy-weight-loss-or-gain-from-eating-disorders/

Roth, G. (1984). *Breaking free from compulsive eating.* New York: Penguin.

Shamblin, G. (2000). *Rise above: God can set you free from your weight problems forever.* Nashville: Nelson.

Shamblin, G. (1997). *The weigh down diet.* New York: Doubleday.

Skorusa, J. (2002). *Staying healthy God's way: Unlocking God's power for health, happiness, & prosperity.* Longwood, FL: Xulon.

Incest

Victorian Government Department of Human Services (2024). *You and your child–a guide for parents of a child who has been sexually abused.* Retrieved January 22, 2024 from https://services.dffh.vic.gov.au/you-and-your-child-guide-parents-child-who-has-been-sexually-abused-word

Overcoming Sexual & Relationship Problems

Arterburn, S. (1992). *Hand-me-down genes and second-hand emotions.* Nashville: Thomas Nelson.
Donovan, M. E., & Ryan, W. P. (1989). *Love blocks: Breaking the patterns that undermine relationships.* New York: Penguin.
Frank, D., & Frank, J. (1990). *When victims marry: Building a stronger marriage by breaking destructive cycles.* San Bernardino, CA: Here's Life.
LaHaye, T. & B. (1976). *The act of marriage: The beauty of sexual love.* Grand Rapids: Zondervan.
McGee, R. S., Graddock, J., & Springle, P. (1990). *Your parents and you: How our parents shape our self-concept, our perception of God and our relationships with others.* USA: Rapha & Word.

Recovery

Allender, D. B. (1990). *The wounded heart: Hope for adult victims of childhood sexual abuse.* Colorado Springs: NavPress.
Arterburn, S., & Felton, J. (1991/1992). *Faith that hurts faith that heals: Understanding the fine line between healthy faith & spiritual abuse.* Nashville: Thomas Nelson.
Bass, E., & Davis, L. (2008). *The courage to heal: A guide for women survivors of child sexual abuse*, 20th anniversary edition. New York, NY: HarperCollins.
Carnes, P. (1993). *A gentle path through the twelve steps (2nd ed.).* Minneapolis: CompCare.
Frank, J. (1987). *A door of hope: Recognizing & resolving the pains of your past.* San Bernardino, CA: Here's Life.

Hemfelt, R., Minirth, F., & Meier, P. (1989). *Love is a choice: Recovery for codependent relationships.* Nashville: Thomas Nelson.

Middleton-Moz, J., & Dwinell, L. (1986). *After the tears: Reclaiming the personal losses of childhood.* Deerfield Beach, FL: Health Communications.

Self-Esteem Issues

Baldwin, S. C. (1989). *If I'm created in God's image why does it hurt to look in the mirror?: A true view of you.* Lynnwood, WA: Aglow.

McGee, R. S. (1998). *The search for significance.* Dallas: Word.

Minirth, F. B., & Meier, P. D. (1994). *Happiness is a choice: The symptoms, causes, and cures of depression (2nd ed.).* Grand Rapids: Baker.

Omartian, S. (1991). *A step in the right direction: Your guide to inner happiness.* Nashville: Thomas Nelson.

Stanley, C. (1999). *Our unmet needs.* Nashville: Thomas Nelson.

Warren, N. C. (1997). *Finding contentment.* Nashville: Thomas Nelson.

Women's Issues

Horton, M., & Byrd, W. (1984). *Keeping your balance: A woman's guide to physical, emotional, and spiritual well-being.* Dallas: Word.

Leman, K. (1987). *Women who try too hard: Breaking the pleaser habits.* Grand Rapids: Fleming H. Revell.

Norwood, R. (1985). *Women who love too much: When you keep wishing and hoping he'll change.* New York: Pocket/St. Martin's.

Omartian, S. (1986). *Stormie.* Eugene, OR: Harvest House.

Omartian, S. (1997). *The power of a praying wife.* Eugene, OR: Harvest House.

Tirabassi, B. (1997). *Let faith change your life.* Nashville: Thomas Nelson.

Walsh, S. (1996). *Honestly.* Grand Rapids: Zondervan.

Educational Curriculum

Langberg, D. (Writer), & American Association of Christian Counselor (Director). (2001a). Sexual abuse/rape/sexual assault [Videotape Lecture]. In Light Learning Institute (Producer), Healthy sexuality. Forest, VA: Director.

Websites

alcohol.org (2024). Helping people recover from alcohol addiction. Available: https://www.alcohol.org/

The American Association of Christian Counselors (2024). *Home Page.* Available: https://aacc.net/

Celebrate Recovery (2024). *Home Page.* Available: https://www.celebraterecovery.com/

Centers.org treatment starts here (2024). *Home Page.* Available: https://www.centers.org/

Christian Association for Psychological Studies (2024). *Home Page.* Available: https://caps.net/

Focus on the Family (2024). *Home Page.* Available: https://www.focusonthefamily.com/

Hope for the Heart (2024). *Home Page.* Available: https://www.hopefortheheart.org/

International Christian Coaching Institute (2024). *Home Page.* Available: https://iccicoaching.com/

Life Recovery Groups (n.d.). *Home Page.* Available: https://liferecoverygroups.com/

National Child Traumatic Stress Network. (2024). *Home Page.* Retrieved January 22, 2024 from https://www.nctsn.org/

Detoxrehabs.org. Dual diagnosis rehabs (2021). Available: https://detoxrehabs.org/dual-diagnosis-rehabs/

RAINN: Rape, Abuse & Incest National Network (2024). *Home Page.* Available: https://rainn.org/

Rehabs.com (2024). Find drug & alcohol rehab options. Available: https://www.rehabs.com/

***

ABOUT THE AUTHOR

Pam Orgeron

Pamela K. Orgeron, M.A., Ed.S., BCCC, ACLC, BCMMHC, formerly Pamela K. Owens (1960-) was born in Ashland, KY. In 1986 she received a B.A. degree in Journalism-Public Relations from Marshall University, Huntington, WV. Also in 1986 Ms. Owens moved to Nashville, TN where she spent over 8 years employed with the Jean and Alexander Heard Library, Vanderbilt University. Before moving back to Kentucky in 2000, she also worked for Harris Publishing and Thomas Nelson Publishers. Ms. Owens received both an M.A. (2003) and an Ed.S. (2009) degree in Adult & Higher Education, Counseling Specialization from Morehead State University, Morehead, KY. Ms. Owens moved back to Nashville in 2009. Since then she has received an Advanced Diploma in Biblical Counseling from Light University and became a Board Certified Christian Counselor, a Board Certified Advanced Christian Life Coach and Board Certified Master Mental Health Coach. In 2010 she married Milton J. Orgeron. She and Milton are General Partners in *ABC's* Ministries, and are members of First Baptist Church, Hendersonville, TN. Mrs. Orgeron also is a certified writer with the Institute of Children's Literature, West Redding, Connecticut. She also is a member of the American Association of Christian Counselors, the International Christian Coaching Association, the International Christian Coaching Institute and the Christian Association of Psychological Studies.

***

Pamela K. Orgeron, M.A., Ed.S., BCCC, ACLC, BCMMHC

Christian Author, Counselor, & Life Coach
General Partner, ABC's Ministries

Contact Pam through the following:
https://www.facebook.com/pam.orgeron
https://www.linkedin.com/in/pamela-orgeron-57873045/

For more information
about ABC's Ministries:
Visit the Website:
https://abcsministries.wordpress.com/

E-mail us at:
abcsministries@yahoo.com

To Learn More about Pam's Journey to Freedom:

In writing *Freedom in Truth: Memoirs of Deliverance and Restoration from Past Abuse and Scandal,* Michaela Maria Marshall (pseudonym), known by her real name as Pam Orgeron, shares her account of being a victim of rape and incest in her early years, also the witnessing of a murder of a friend by one of her perpetrators who was attempting to molest the murder victim's little sister. Ms. Marshall also experienced years of physical and emotional abuse.

The author's purpose in writing *Freedom in Truth*, like the purpose of *Overcoming Generational Curses*, is to follow the Holy Spirit's direction to enable the principles expressed in 2 Corinthians 1:3-4 to be lived out in her life. If by sharing what happened to her will spare other victims experiencing similar incidents from having to be further victimized by families trying to cover up similar tragedies, more concerned about family reputations than the feelings and needs of the victims involved, then her mission has been accomplished.

Webpage: https://freedom-in-truth.com/

Available for purchase:
https://www.amazon.com/Freedom-Truth-Memoirs-Deliverance-Restoration/dp/1462412556
https://www.barnesandnoble.com/w/freedom-in-truth-michaela-maria-marshall/1131124975
other online bookstores

Book Review: https://www.kirkusreviews.com/book-reviews/michaela-maria-marshall/freedom-in-truth-memoirs-of-deliverance-and-restor/

OTHER BOOKS ABOUT OVERCOMING PAST ABUSE BY PAM ORGERON:

Why Didn't They Hear Us?

Do you hear the children cry?

Are you ready to become a part of the solution to the problem of children being unheard? If so, this book is for you!

"'We Survived' is probably the best resource I have seen on the subject and is a "must read" for mental health professionals and those on pastoral staffs. Anyone who provides help to others would find this book helpful. The voices of the victims themselves give authenticity and will help the reader better understand sexual abuse. For any victims, survivors and/or offenders of sexual abuse, I recommend they read this book to aid them in the healing process."–We Survived Sexual Abuse! You Can Too! Preface; Eugene (Gene) H. Benedict MA LPC-S, San Antonio, Texas.

www.ingramcontent.com/pod-product-compliance
Lightning Source LLC
Chambersburg PA
CBHW052143070526
44585CB00017B/1959